VILLA GARDENS
OF THE
MEDITERRANEAN

VILLA GARDENS
OF THE
MEDITERRANEAN

FROM THE ARCHIVES OF
COUNTRY LIFE

KATHRYN BRADLEY-HOLE

AURUM PRESS

To the memory of R C G, P H L G and F C
Also to S P A N A and The Brooke Hospital, two splendid organisations
which do much to help distressed working horses, donkeys and mules in
the Mediterranean region

First published in Great Britain 2006 by Aurum Press Limited
25 Bedford Avenue, London WC1B 3AT
www.aurumpress.co.uk

Text copyright © 2006 by Kathryn Bradley-Hole
Photographs copyright © *Country Life* Picture Library

The right of Kathryn Bradley-Hole to be identified as author of this work has been
asserted by her in accordance with the Copyright, Designs and Patents Act, 1988.

A catalogue record for this book is available from the British Library.

ISBN 1 84513 124 X
10 9 8 7 6 5 4 3 2 1
2010 2009 2008 2007 2006

Design by James Campus
Originated, printed and bound in Singapore by CS Graphics

Frontispiece: Villa Hanbury, by Andrew Lawson.
Front endpaper: St Peter's Basilica, Rome, from the gateway of Villa Doria Pamphilj, by Charles Latham.
Rear endpaper: A formal garden at Lou Sueil, by G. R. Ballance.

THE COUNTRY LIFE PICTURE LIBRARY

The *Country Life* Picture Library holds a complete set of prints made from its
negatives, and a card index to the subjects, usually recording the name of the photographer and the date of the photographs catalogued, together with a separate index of
photographers. It also holds a complete set of *Country Life* and various forms of
published indices to the magazine. The Library may be visited by appointment, and
prints of any negatives it holds can be supplied by post.

For further information, please contact the Librarian, Camilla Costello, at *Country
Life*, King's Reach Tower, Stamford Street, London SE1 9LS (*Tel:* 020 7261 6337).

ACKNOWLEDGEMENTS

My special thanks go to Clare Howell, consultant editor for Aurum Press, and
James Campus, who has designed this book with great sympathy for the subjects and
photographs. Also to my husband Christopher for his enthusiasm and support, to
Karen Ings and Piers Burnett at Aurum, Camilla Costello and her staff at the *Country
Life* Picture Library, and Clive Aslet, editor of *Country Life*. The magazine's talented
photographers, both past and present, are numerous and their names are listed below.

Particular thanks go to my hosts in Algiers, Brian and Annie Stewart, who did so
much to make my visit there not only possible but also immensely rewarding, and to
Rachida Benyahia and Osman Benchérif, who assisted greatly through their own
contacts. I am grateful to the owners, residents and staff associated with the properties
in this book and many other helpers along the way, including: the staff of the Royal
Horticultural Society's Lindley Library; the tourist boards of Spain, Nice and Èze;
Stephen Bucknall, Fernando Caruncho, Cali Doxiadis, Robert and Sibyl Erdman,
Heidi Gildemeister, Mark Griffiths, Peter Hinwood, Valerie Humphrey, Elisabeth
Joppek, Juan and Carmen Leña, Michael Likierman, Andrew Lyndon-Skeggs,
Sofia Bosco Martinez de Aguilar, Nigel Massey, David Messias, Olivier Picard, Sylvaine
Poitau, Lex and Antoinette Redelé-Dutilh, Akira and Mari Urabe, William Waterfield,
Robin Whalley, Yann and Joanna Zedde.

CHAPTER OPENING QUOTATIONS

France: Edith Wharton, *The House of Mirth*, Macmillan & Co., London, 1905.
Italy: Axel Munthe, *The Story of San Michele*, John Murray, London, 1929.
Algeria: Robert Hichens, *The Garden of Allah*, Methuen & Co., London, 1904.
Greece: Sophie Atkinson, *An Artist in Corfu*, Herbert & Daniel, London, 1911.
Spain: Graham Greene, *Monsignor Quixote*, Random House, London, 1982.
Portugal: William Beckford, *Recollections of an Excursion to the Monasteries of Alcobaca
and Batalha with his Original Journal of 1794*, Centaur Press, London, 1972.

PICTURE CREDITS

El Bardo: Frederick Evans (b/w); Sylvaine Poitau (colour). *Campagne Montfeld:*
Sylvaine Poitau. *Casa da Insua:* Alex Starkey. *Casa de Pilatos:* Alex Starkey (pages 186–7
and 189); Alex Ramsay (pages 188, 190 and 191). *Casa Postigo:* Jerry Harpur.
Cavogallo: Mark Fiennes. *Les Collettes:* Tim Imrie-Tait. *Dar El Ouard:* Sylvaine Poitau.
Djenan-Ali-Raïs: Sylvaine Poitau. *Djenan El Mufti:* Frederick Evans. *Emerald Park:*
Sylvaine Poitau. *Flor da Rosa:* Mark Fiennes. *Gastouri:* Jerry Harpur. *Gildemeister
Gardens:* Nicolas Sapieha. *Isola Madre:* Mark Fiennes. *La Léopolda:* G. R. Ballance.
Lou Sueil: G. R. Ballance. *Moratalla:* June Buck. *La Mortella:* Jerry Harpur.
Oued-El-Kalaï: Frederick Evans. *Sainte-Claire le Château:* G. R. Ballance (b/w);
Vivian Russell (colour). *Sant' Antonio:* Simon Upton. *Santa Chiara:* Jerry Harpur.
Serre de la Madone: Sylvaine Poitau. *Villa Balbianello:* Val Corbett. *Villa Cypris:*
G. R. Ballance. *Villa Doria Pamphilj:* Charles Latham. *Villa Gregoriana:* Simon Upton.
Villa Hanbury: G. R. Ballance (b/w); Andrew Lawson (colour). *Villa Île de France:*
Sylvaine Poitau. *Villa Maryland:* photographer unknown. *Villa Noailles:* Vivian Russell.
Villa Sylvia: photographer unknown.

CONTENTS

The Mediterranean. Azure skies; white sails on blue waters; bleached and craggy landscapes redolent with the volatile scent of pine, rosemary, lavender and sage,

their flowers foraged by bees. Olive trees shimmer in clouds of cascading silver and the tethered dog barks alone in the farmyard; the invisible nightingale trills among the lentisc; and goat bells clang and tinkle on the stony hillside.

Against this captivating backdrop people build villas and make gardens, as they have done since time immemorial. The historian Christopher Thacker has neatly encapsulated the foundations of Mediterranean garden-making: 'When man first felt that there was a difference between the "atmosphere" surrounding one place and another; that some spot possessed a mysterious quality; that some mysterious or tragic event had left an emotional effect on the nearby rocks and trees and streams; that a remote locality might possess a "spirit" of its own, a *genius loci*: at this moment, man was close to creating a "sacred grove".' From that point, the creation of gardens was a natural – and unnatural – progression, whose stories have been brilliantly told in many books.

This book is not a history of Mediterranean gardens, but rather a celebration of them, as seen through the unique eyes of *Country Life* magazine for more than a hundred years. It is also my personal selection, a mere thirty-three gardens drawn from an archive of more than 150 in the Mediterranean region specially photographed for the magazine since its beginnings in 1897.

In choosing the gardens that follow, my aim has been to research and present as wide a range as possible, while taking the irresistible opportunity to revisit at length some of the extraordinary horticultural treasures of the 1900–30 era. We will never again see the like of set-pieces such as Lou Sueil, created at vast expense by Consuelo Vanderbilt Balsan through

the 1920s, or the pristine botanical collection of La Mortola (Villa Hanbury) as it was in its pre-1939 glory days. And when Charles Latham photographed the Villa Doria Pamphilj on the outskirts of Rome *circa* 1900, its priceless antique statuary was still intact within a beautifully tended park, though most of its vast grounds are in a parlous state today, with a motorway rushing through the middle. At El Bardo and Oued-El-Kalaï in Algeria, the luminous Edwardian photographs by the great Frederick Evans reveal Ottoman gardens of rare distinction, before twentieth-century conflicts and earthquakes took their toll in the region. They also convey an atmosphere of leisure and hand-nurtured refinement that has universally disappeared, not only from the traffic-choked streets of modern Algiers.

✣   ✣   ✣

'There will be a great foregathering of English folk on the Riviera this Eastertide,' wrote H. Avray Tipping in festive mood in *Country Life*'s edition of 30 March 1912, '... for it is then that the statue of Queen Victoria is to be unveiled at Nice and that of King Edward at Cannes. Then, too, the harbour of Villefranche is to be the scene of a meeting of the fleets of the *entente cordiale* group, France acting as hostess to her Russian and English friends.'

The eager flag-waving that Easter weekend can be imagined, yet the smiles on those rosy-cheeked faces were soon to freeze over for a long time. Back in Southampton, the *Titanic*, pride of the White Star Line, had been gaily dressed with flags and pennants for Good Friday, 5 April, but by sunrise on Monday 15 April, *Titanic* had struck an iceberg and plunged to the icy depths of the Atlantic. Among the 1,500 people who went down

Left: *The deep-blue waters of the Mediterranean, framed by the branches of olives and aromatic pines, seen from the gardens of Cavogallo in the Southern Peloponnese.*

with her were members of many families who had helped to create the myth of the Riviera of the belle époque.

Since the 1860s and the arrival of the railways, fabulous gardens had flourished all over the Riviera, but in the new century storms were brewing. Kaiser Wilhelm II had for some years been using his good arm to rattle a sabre at his British cousins. Finally, when the boiling magma of imperial rivalries erupted into the First World War, the Riviera became an emergency sanctuary under the umbrella pines. Its hotels were turned into hospitals and its airy sanitoria housed wounded conscripts alongside the more familiar gatherings of consumptives. Riviera conversation that had for fifty years and longer been focused on 'lungs and anemones' shifted to limbs and armouries.

Yet during the years of the 1914–18 war, *Country Life*'s few features on the old Moorish gardens of Algiers and Andalucía brought a little southern warmth and some respite into the lives of its readers between more pressing stories, such as how to increase your potato yield, and how the Army was acquiring 'remounts', or fresh horses, for the unending hell of the Western Front.

Algiers, on the Mediterranean's southern shore, had been the favourite winter resort of countless well-heeled Britons in the mid- and late nineteenth century; since at least the 1850s, many British families (and some Americans) owned property on the fringes of this fascinating city; others took leases on villas for the season, or stayed in one of the growing number of hotels. Nearly all of them were based in the districts of Mustapha Supérieur and El-Biar, some 3 miles south-west of the ancient Arab city. There the air was clear and fresh, the green hills were watered by countless springs, and the sparkling views over the Bay of Algiers were utterly captivating.

The neighbourhood of Mustapha was also where Algeria's own princes and corsair rulers had been settled for centuries, prior to French domination and colonisation in 1830, and they had built their country estates in all the best locations. Eugène Fromentin observed in *Une Année dans le Sahel* (1857): 'The Turkish houses rise here and there, ... so well surrounded and isolated by trees that they have the air of each one possessing a park. All are built in picturesque situations on the wooded incline of the Sahel, and all have a grand and beautiful view of the sea.' He noted, however: 'Today, without exception, they are occupied by Europeans ...'

Right: *By the 1920s, Villa Monbrillant's garden at Cannes was thought old-fashioned, with its palm-studded lawn framed by an old pepper tree.*

Below: *This photograph from the 1920s reveals the former splendour of the majolica-tiled pergola at Santa Chiara, Naples, shaded by abundant grapevines.*

Many of those Europeans came to paint the scenery, its exotic vegetation, its camels, its curious architecture and indigenous people shrouded in veils. Orientalist painters concocted erotic scenes set in harem courtyards. Others came to Algiers to shoot what was once plentiful game – partridges, hares, snipe, wild ducks and wild boars near the city; lions and panthers still attracted 'the more adventurous spirits southward', suggested L. G. Séguin, author of *Walks in Algiers*, in 1878. (Consequently, the magnificent black-maned barbary lion was extinct in the wild by 1922.)

Even more visitors were, like the *hivernants* (winterers) on the Riviera (and Malta, Málaga and Naples), looking for relief from tuberculosis; the 1899 *Illustrated Guide to Algiers* devoted several pages to descriptions of hospitals and gathered the endorsements of a dozen doctors on the benign air found in 'the promised land of consumptives'. (It was not a universal cure, but the change of air and climate and removal from everyday sources of stress seemed to help many patients, though consumption continued to be a major killer in the Western world until the development of streptomycin in the 1940s.) The Hôtel d'Orient hosted subscription balls to amuse its clients, though it was understood that 'unmarried ladies under thirty, and gentlemen whose dancing powers are not impeded by asthma, are at a premium'.

Among those who had taken long leases or made outright purchases of property on the outskirts of Algiers, there were many keen gardeners who did not wish to sit out the winter at home when they could be making a garden in North Africa, with its more exotic flora. The villas of many residents were sensitively restored by the English architect Benjamin Bucknall, who lived in Algiers from 1877 until his death in 1895. In the early twentieth century, other exotic destinations (such as Biskra and Cairo) beckoned, but 'the Torquay of North Africa' still attracted a loyal following until the 1930s.

What became of the British gardens in Algiers in the intervening years, in a country which has been torn apart by terrible wars and completely out of bounds to recent generations of travellers? In 2005 I went there to find out. The stories of some gardens are revealed here for the first time; others for the first time in eighty or ninety years.

✣   ✣   ✣

Since the earliest days of *Country Life*, plenty of Mediterranean influences have filtered back into English gardens. Throughout the Edwardian era there were numerous articles about pergolas and how to plant them and few gardens designed by Lutyens and/or Jekyll did not feature a vine-garlanded pergola somewhere in the plan. Over many years Miss Jekyll wrote in various journals about the plants she had admired abroad: the winter irises and wild clematis in Algiers; the geraniums and Madonna lilies in Italy; aromatic herbs in Greece. A 1920 feature on Ashford Chace in Hampshire (completed in 1912 to designs by W. F. Unsworth and H. Inigo Triggs) showed a courtyard in unabashed Moorish style, complete with arcaded gallery, Arab fountain and a 'maze' channel. It replicated those in the old gardens of Algiers and Andalucía that Unsworth had painstakingly measured up and drawn to scale on his trips abroad.

In the 1920s, plantsmanship began to be the dominant focus in the garden articles, rather than design – and this remained the case through most of the twentieth century. Spectacular gardens such as those of Edith Wharton at Hyères and the Hanburys at Ventimiglia were discussed in terms of their winter and spring plant content above all else. But another change was on the horizon: in the 1930s, fashions began to shift away from winter sunshine to summer. On the Riviera, for example, and in the Italian Lakes, film-star-inspired suntans could be cultivated during sociable sports such as sailing, tennis, golf and even just straightforward sunbathing – the latter pastime would have been unthinkable to the previous generation.

The garden designer Russell Page (1906–85) was among the people who articulated the changeover as it happened: 'People installed themselves in their villas for three [winter] months and Cap Ferrat, like Cannes, was mainly colonised by the garden-loving English,' he recalled of the Riviera scene in the 1930s. 'When I went back to garden on the Riviera in 1947 all this had changed. Restrictions had eliminated the English colony, their villas were either bombed or deserted or had been bought by the French, the Belgians or the Swiss. The South of France is now a summer resort and new gardens must be mainly designed for summer. People open their houses for ten days at Christmas and perhaps for as long at Easter, but the real season runs from June to September. This makes gardening an exercise in prolongation.'

Since the arrival of colour photography in *Country Life* in the last quarter of the twentieth century, coverage of Mediterranean gardens has extended into Spain, Greece and Portugal, reflecting the broader holiday- and second-home ownership trends observed by Russell Page. These days, every villa needs its swimming pool, though siting it still seems a challenge, especially since present-day plots are so small. In the 1950s, Page believed that 'a swimming pool is most satisfactory when treated as part of the general composition but isolated as a separate compartment ... best concealed, or partly concealed, by wall or hedge.' Hiding the pool, as the Victorians did the piano's legs lest they offend, is one way; but today's garden designers have brought the swimming pool 'out of the closet', and, though this book is more concerned with garden content, contemporary pictures rightly include the pool as well as the pergola.

Kathryn Bradley-Hole

Above: *A doorway in old Algiers garlanded with spring-flowering wisteria.* Country Life *published this exquisite watercolour by Ella du Cane in 1927.*

Below: *A traditional garden seat, one of many in the grounds of Dar El Ouard, Algiers, which are gaily decorated with tiles.*

Left: *The bold form of a white-flowered Brugmansia, or angel's trumpet, and clipped cypresses at Villa Île de France, Saint-Jean-Cap-Ferrat.*

The little path wound on and on between two running rills of water, which slipped incessantly away under the broad and yellow-tipped leaves of dwarf palms, making a music so faint that it was more like a remembered sound in the mind than one which slid upon the ear. On either hand towered a jungle of trees brought to this home in the desert from all parts of the world. ... The hibiscus lifted languidly its frail and rosy cup, and the red gold oranges gleamed amid leaves that looked as if they had been polished by an attentive fairy.

Robert Hichens, *The Garden of Allah*

Algeria

An Edwardian photograph reveals strelitzias and fragrant pansies surrounding an old Moorish octagonal fountain in the gardens of El Bardo, where a light breeze ripples the fronds of jungly palm trees.

OUED-EL-KALAÏ, EL-BIAR

These rare photographs of Villa Oued-El-Kalaï form part of a mini-series taken by the renowned photographer Frederick Evans (1853–1943). They are believed to date from the very early years of the twentieth century, when he was doing a significant amount of work for *Country Life*, particularly on French châteaux. Evans's Algerian photographs, as much as his better-known work, reveal his complete mastery of light, composition and atmosphere. Though its companions in the series (Djenan El Mufti, *page 20*, and El Bardo, *page 26*) were published in 1915 with informative articles written by Inigo Triggs, the well-known Edwardian architect and landscape designer, Oued-El-Kalaï seems never to have materialised in a magazine feature – perhaps because editorial space in *Country Life* was increasingly being devoted to Allied efforts on the Western Front as the First World War progressed. It is an interesting property, however, not least because it played a fascinating walk-on part in the North Africa campaign in the Second World War, being the

home, for a while, of Duff Cooper, British Ambassador in Algiers in the first eight months of 1944.

Like so many of the properties on the stream-riven heights of El-Biar and neighbouring Mustapha Supérieur, villages overlooking the bay of Algiers, Oued-El-Kalaï, in the fashionable Chemin Beaurepaire, was an original Ottoman summer residence, perched on the hillside with glorious views and set in a rich green landscape. Its neighbours included the elegant Villa Montfeld (*see page 36*) and Campagne du Pavillon, which for many years had been the winter home of Barbara Leigh Smith Bodichon, the painter and founder of Girton College, Cambridge, whom a young Gertrude Jekyll had stayed with in the

Right: *Frederick Evans's luminous photographs of Oued-El-Kalaï, taken 100 years ago, convey the luxuriance of Algerian gardens in the days when keen English owners spent the winter tending their well-planted domains. Note the excellent condition of both plants and paths.*

Below: *A handsome avenue of cypresses lined the drive and gave it welcome shade.*

winter of 1873–74. And a stone's-throw away there was the Villa Sidi Aloui, which had been the home of Sir Lambert Playfair, the British consul-general in the last three decades of the nineteenth century, that halcyon period of leisurely British interest and artistic pursuits in Algiers.

There can be no more telling descriptions of El-Kalaï than those related by Lady Diana Cooper in her remarkable wartime memoirs, *Trumpets from the Steep*. Though it had been one of the premier villas occupied by the overwintering English during the belle époque, with a richly planted and immaculately maintained garden, by 1944 it had clearly seen better days: 'We turned into a very beautiful, measureless *Belle au Bois Dormant* demesne. As far as eye could see was jungle of palm and cypress-covered hills, green as jade. We came to a Moorish door, a courtyard, hammam and tiles, cypress and arches. The home of Omar, I thought, Jamshid's palace ...'

The Sleeping Beauty dream was shattered, however, when the Coopers ventured indoors: 'Gloomy darkness, paralysing cold and dusty, musty squalor. The style was ragged palmist – a dingy junk shop ...' What piqued her most of all was that the military and foreign attachés all appeared to be occupying more graciously maintained villas in the neighbourhood, while the Coopers had been forced to make do with 'brothel-like' sitting rooms, 'hubble-bubbles green with verdigris, heavy brass beds thinly overlaid, unvalanced and equally green, exposing cracked chamber-pots, baths brownly stained, lavatory pans not describable, no looking-glasses or curtains, no washerwoman (there being no soap), no anything, sans, sans, sans'.

Arriving in the middle of winter and in the late stages of the war had not helped, for the shops were empty of any supplies worth having and the nights were so cold that Lady Diana slept in her fur coat. The villa had a garden, though, and with the arrival of February and North Africa's early spring, bulbs shot up and golden mimosa burst joyfully into bloom, and the packing cases arrived with the furnishings, china, glass and paraphernalia essential to diplomatic life. Things looked much brighter. The 'many shaded glades and hills' of the domain provided tolerable camping for stranded English civilians, who helped war prisoners to tend the garden. 'Some evenings at dusk Duff and I walk round our Arabian property,' Diana wrote, in more cheerful mood. 'It's huge, beautiful, romantic, and the seasons will bring flowers and new fruits.'

Indeed they did. There were armfuls of arum lilies and large bunches of fragrant freesias to be picked every morning, as well as apple and orange blossoms, pansies, daisies, night-scented stocks and emerging cascades of mauve wisteria. Judas trees burst into magenta blossoms along their branches and trunks, rapidly followed by the violet clouds of jacaranda. A menagerie had been assembled, starting with a milk cow, then a pair of strutting peacocks and a tame though short-lived gazelle; later additions included a silver cat and a nuzzling donkey. Guests were many, and not always the worst kind of officials, who had to be tolerated

Arum lilies thrive in an octagonal marble pool featuring a handsome carved marble fountain. Note the decorative edging tiles enclosing the surrounding flowerbeds.

more or less politely – many brighter sparks sailed through, including Martha Gellhorn, Joyce Grenfell, Evelyn Waugh, the British war artist Major Carr and French novelist André Gide.

In times of sadness, there were the mountains behind Algiers and their primeval cedars to escape to. In every gorge were crowds of pink oleanders, ripened figs falling from the trees, and even, somewhat symbolically, olive trees – under whose boughs lay menacing piles of shells, bombs and other munitions of varying sizes.

With the arrival of summer 1944, the Coopers would not have very much longer to stay in the 'once hated house' that had rapidly bewitched Diana and become 'a palace of two worlds – of earth and of heaven'. The second of September was the proposed departure date. During the punishing heat of August, meals were no longer taken under the garden loggia but indoors, in the windowless Arab-pillared hall. Even so, outdoors the vines were green as English spring, the trees continued to blossom 'as if their feet were in water' – which they probably were, for El-Biar is the place of the wells, its greenery resulting

from an above-average quantity of springs which had fed the neighbourhood's gardens and orchards for centuries.

Today, the villa Oued-El-Kalai is still there, forming part of the American Embassy complex and necessarily enclosed by high walls, razor wire and the trappings of high security. Frederick Evans's luminous 100-year-old photographs reveal it in the context of a very different world – different even from the one that the Coopers had inhabited thirty years later. But they show enough to make us realise what a wrench it must have been for the irrepressible Diana Cooper to leave: 'My tears could not be stopped, and they had to be silent ones, for they were out of place and hysterical on so happy a day. They would not stop and for many years talk of Algiers would summon them back in my eyes, to everyone's amusement.'

Above: *The triple-arched loggia was engulfed in treasured potted plants, both inside and out.*

Right: *A raised pergola walk running from the house into the gardens. Below it, the next level of garden featured flowerbeds brimming with anemones, cinerarias and fragrant wallflowers, edged with dwarf hedging and punctuated by standard yuccas and palms.*

DJENAN EL MUFTI, MUSTAPHA SUPÉRIEUR

Filippo Pananti's account of his experiences of Algiers – including a period of slavery after being captured by Barbary corsairs off the coast of Sardinia in 1813 – caused a sensation when it was first published in 1817. There were several editions and translations, including an English one in 1830. It was by no means the first description of slavery, or even the goriest – enslavement of European Christians captured at sea and brought to the Barbary lands had been going on for nearly three hundred years – but it helped to foster widespread approval of the French military invasion and colonisation of Algeria.

As long ago as 1665, Emanuele d'Aranda had written in his *History of Algiers*, 'In this piratical city the miseries of slavery have consumed the lives of six hundred thousand Christians since the year 1536'. Pananti's version described how 'Some, like the beasts of burden, are employed in carrying stones and wood for any public buildings that may be going on. These are usually in chains, and justly considered as the most unfortunate among their oppressed brethren. ... Made to sink wells and clean

Above: *The tiled approach from the house to the Fountain Court. An aspidistra, the beloved evergreen of Victorian households, thrives in the elegant glazed pot near the door.*

Left: *A view across the Fountain Court. The extensive tiling on the walls was probably added during refurbishments by Benjamin Bucknall in the late 1870s, since an earlier painting shows this courtyard as largely untiled.*

sewers, yoked with the ass and the mule, hundreds die miserably every year. The slightest offence is punished with two hundred blows on the feet or back, and when exhausted or sick, the wretched sufferers are abandoned like dogs by the roadside.' So there was a poignancy in an Englishman's inscription among the decorations at Djenan El Mufti: '*John Robson, with my hand this 3rd day Jany in the year 1692.*' Like many other private villas and public buildings, the builders and craftsmen were Christian slaves, and while some achieved freedom and prosperity, many more died in conditions of great suffering.

Two centuries on from John Robson's inscription, Djenan El Mufti (the garden of the councillor, or mullah), built for Hadj-Chaban Pasha, was in British ownership, the property of Mr and Mrs Thomas Glen Arthur. Mrs Arthur had long been familiar with Algiers – her grandfather, Sir Peter Coats, of the famous Scottish thread-and-textile manufacturing family, had owned Campagne du Sahel, one of the finest estates in Mustapha Supérieur. Her husband, Thomas, also in the Scottish textile industry, was a keen collector of fine art and a lay member of the Glasgow Art Club. After Thomas's death in 1907, his widow stayed on in Algiers, and her home became the social hub of the neighbourhood when the English Club (at Emerald Park; *see page 32*) folded.

Even a hundred years ago, the villa was regarded as a precious survivor from the seventeenth century, since so many old Moorish houses had been plundered and destroyed. Others had not survived the earthquakes that plague this tectonically active region. That these photographs of 100 years ago show the house and grounds in such good condition was due to the efforts of the English architect Benjamin Bucknall, who settled in Algiers in 1877 and stayed there until his death in 1895.

Bucknall restored many of the old Arab houses that had been in a parlous state and also built new ones in the Ottoman style, which were much admired for their conformity to the old traditions. (In the hilly suburb of El-Biar, where most of his work was carried out, a street, Chemin Bucknall, was named in recognition of his work, though post-Independence, in 1962, its name was changed.)

Set on the hillside facing north-east and overlooking the bay of Algiers, Djenan El Mufti was built in the middle of a fine park, with long terraces streaming out south-eastwards along the contours of the hill. These terraces were fashioned into a series of formal gardens, the upper garden beside the house having a parterre arrangement of no less than twenty large beds edged with rosemary, its central path ornamented by Moorish fountains at intervals.

Springing out of the terracotta-red earth were diminutive flowers and

bulbs under the luxuriant foliage of subtropical trees. In 1915, the architect and garden designer Inigo Triggs praised its 'Magnificent bougainvilleas in masses of richest purple or brick red colouring', making such a good contrast to the sombre greens of cypress and palm, and admired 'the scarlet hibiscus with its almost transparent flowers, the strelitzia, reminiscent of the gay plumage of the parrot, daturas, Japanese medlars [or loquats, *Eriobotrya japonica*], bamboos, prickly pears draped and festooned with *Clematis cirrhosa*, and the brugmansia with great white trumpets'. This was clearly a garden in the spirit of Robert Hichens' 1904 bestseller, *The Garden of Allah*, a novel which boosted tourism in Algeria in much the same way as Peter Mayle's *A Year in Provence* swelled the ranks of holidaymakers in the South of France.

Also in the upper garden were many palms, including ones producing dates; also cycads, and poinsettias grown as standards, reliably producing their scarlet plumage at Christmas-time. Trumpets of crimson and vivid-blue morning glory scrambled through trees and shrubs. Though the layout of the garden was very formal, the abundance of casually arranged, well-watered plants and the stepped nature of the terrain made it appear less so.

The middle terrace featured a very long gravelled walk through a citrus orchard, where vast parallel beds were filled with oranges, lemons and mandarins. At the farthest end, the orchard terminated in an arcaded loggia, with five arches held aloft on barleytwist marble columns. Under the central arch was an exquisitely tiled wall fountain pouring into a basin, which then overflowed into a 'puzzle maze' carved out of a single slab of marble. 'This form of grooved slab known as a puzzle fountain was a favourite device in the old Moorish gardens,' wrote Triggs. 'Rose leaves were allowed to float along the tiny current and took the place of dice in whiling away a lazy hour among the fair inhabitants of the hareem. It was a curious idea, found in the gardens of the Alcázar at Seville, and as far back as the fifteenth century. Illustrations of the Romaunt of the Rose show how such water channels running from garden to garden were made the carriers of written messages.'

Between the orchard's end and the puzzle fountain, a gravelled courtyard had seats and tables arranged under bowers of climbing roses,

Above: *A traditional Moorish puzzle fountain carved out of a single slab of marble. It was created as the centrepiece in the summerhouse of another elegant courtyard, located at the far end of an orchard of orange, lemon and mandarin trees.*

Right: *A wellhead in the lower gardens, where planting included spring-flowering magnolias and thick bands of violas along the path edge.*

while the central feature was a tiled square pool where goldfish darted among the reeds of papyrus, but you had to stroll back, down the length of the orchard, to reach the lower gardens. There, near the villa, a majolica-tiled stairway led further down the hillside through carpets of wild irises. Further paths and steps edged with violets led the way between more palms, succulent agaves, spring-flowering magnolias and general botanical abundance to the water garden, a natural pond.

Back at the house, there was a fine example of a Moorish courtyard, lavishly tiled and cloistered. We know that Bucknall was involved in upgrading and possibly even extending the villa at some stage between 1877 and 1895, but it now seems certain that he installed the great quantity of tiled decoration in Djenan El Mufti's courtyards. Prior to Mr and Mrs Glen Arthur residing at the property, it had been the winter residence of another British family, the Smith Barrys of County Cork, Ireland. Arthur Hugh Smith Barry (1843–1925), the 1st and last Baron Barrymore, and his first wife, Lady Mary Frances Wyndham-Quin, daughter of the 3rd Earl of Dunraven, were charmingly painted, as casually as any Victorian portraiture would permit, sitting in the shade of the Fountain Court at Djenan El Mufti with their young daughter, Geraldine (and pet pug dog), in 1876. At that stage, there were few tiles to be seen in the courtyard, though everything else except its orange tree (which was later replaced by a palm) seems much the same as in *Country Life*'s photographs.

But perhaps it is worth concluding with the words of Maurice Magnus, an educated American of German descent, whose recollections of a fleeting visit in 1916 capture the spirit of the place better than anything else:

'Next day, Easter Sunday, the Consul and his wife and I were invited to Mrs Arthur's whose house is supposed to be the most beautiful Arab house in Algiers. It stands in a large magnificent garden filled with the most luxuriant flowers. I shall not make the mistake of mentioning what flowers, as Robert Hichens did. He filled Mrs Arthur's garden, in a chapter of one of his books, with rhododendrons, and when she wrote asking if he did not know that rhododendrons didn't grow in Africa, he changed the chapter in the second edition.

'Mrs Arthur was a very beautiful old lady, and very interesting, with a great deal of charm. Her house was wonderful. There was nothing in it that was not purely Arab, and yet it had all the comfort and luxury of an English home. The open courtyard with its fountain, the banks of flowers, the exquisite Arab furniture and gorgeous hangings, the wonderful collection of Arab weapons and ornaments, made one feel as if Aladdin's Lamp had been rubbed. She told me that one day, two Arab women visited her and begged her to allow them to see again the house of their childhood. She was most interested, naturally, and showed them about, and inquired how the house had looked when they had occupied it; and then she changed it accordingly, so that the house was not only Arab in general aspect, but also in detail and atmosphere. She told me that she intended to leave the house to the State as a museum.'

The lower gardens included a natural spring-fed pond, reached via steps down the hill and neatly rolled paths. The grafted and carefully pruned weeping tree reminds us that this was a garden much prized by the horticultural community of Algiers.

EL BARDO, MUSTAPHA SUPÉRIEUR

In 1888, having hired a phaeton for a day's exploration of Algiers, Edith Wharton and her travelling companions coasted through the meandering streets of Mustapha Supérieur. 'We passed the summer palace of the Governor, getting a glimpse of well-kept gardens through the gateways,' she noted. Had the young Mrs Wharton not been painfully unwell for those few days of her sojourn in Algiers, she might have been encouraged to call on M. Pierre Joret, the cultured owner of the nearby property known as El Bardo. This remarkable eighteenth-century villa, built for Prince Sidi Ben Hadj Omar, exiled from Tunisia, was taken over by the French after the conquest of 1830 and continued in various French ownerships until it was bought by Ali Bey, Agha of Biskra, in 1875. Under his guidance, restoration of its Moorish features and tilework began to be carried out by the architect Benjamin Bucknall; it seems that this was one of the first of Bucknall's Algerian projects (he settled in Algiers in 1875).

In 1879, Pierre Joret bought El Bardo from Ali Bey and continued the job of restoring the lost grandeur of its Ottoman days with great enthusiasm. He also filled its interiors with precious collections of art, musical instruments, porcelain and fine fabrics. El Bardo was inherited by Joret's sister after his death, but in 1926 the Joret family generously decided to donate the property to the Algerian government to ensure its preservation in the face of all the new-build and demolition going on in the neighbourhood.

Country Life's luminous photographs of El Bardo, taken probably some years prior to the First World War but published in 1915, concentrated on its elegant courtyards, originally the exclusive domain of the harem. Around the courtyards there are more extensive gardens of mature trees and raised flowerbeds, and a long carriage drive linking the old villa to the serpentine street that is these days known as rue Franklin D. Roosevelt. A flight of steps, with the risers picked out in patterned tiles, leads from the driveway to a heavy, nail-studded door into the harem's apartments and courtyards.

The main court, a summer salon, focuses on a central octagonal-shaped pool and fountain. To one side, a three-arched loggia which was, and is, beautifully tiled, led at one end through a carved and panelled

Above left: *Detail of fine tilework in the courtyard, where restorations are in progress.*

Above right: *The entrance to the Harem Court, which is completely enclosed.*

Left: *The courtyard of the harem, as it is today, now forms part of the Bardo Museum. Though the towering cypress tree looks ancient, it was only planted in the 1920s, replacing a different tree.*

door – originally painted with flowers, though they are now very faded – into the private apartment of the favourite. Low raised beds either side of this courtyard have long been planted with strelitzias – *S. alba* and *S. reginae* – though Inigo Triggs, who wrote about El Bardo in 1915, pointed out that few flowers were cultivated in harem courtyards: '... those that find a place are chosen for their bright colour and the sweetness of their scent – roses, lilies, jasmine, violets, pinks and geraniums. Once planted, they are allowed to ramp over trellis and pergola without restraint.'

One of the particular features of El Bardo, just visible in the old photograph below, was its collection of traditional Algerian earthenware pots, or water jars. They were characteristically slender at the bottom but bulging into round bellies in the upper half and decorated with the age-old patterns of the indigenous Kabyle tribespeople. As garden pots they were set upon broad saucers and planted with seasonal flowers, such as pelargoniums, but their great rarity today might be accounted for, in part, by the ease with which such a shape could topple over and crack. Barbara Leigh Smith Bodichon, the English painter, was so taken with them that she had some examples sent to the South Kensington (now Victoria and Albert) Museum. Even in the mid-

nineteenth century they were being replaced everywhere by what she dismissed as 'hideous and cheap French earthenware'. Beside the Fountain Court is the Women's Court, with a large rectangular pool and another covered loggia, larger than its neighbour, and which the early pictures show as being furnished with banquettes, cushions, rugs and many potted plants.

For Victorian and Edwardian travellers to Algiers who were of a creative inclination – such as Barbara Bodichon, Gertrude Jekyll, Inigo Triggs and his partner architect, W. F. Unsworth – it was the singular artistic life of the place and the quality of its surviving old buildings which gave it the edge over the newer Mediterranean resorts. As Triggs explained in his article of 1915: 'Arab writers tell us that the private houses of Damascus were built after the fashion of the later Roman houses, whereas in Persia, and especially in Baghdad, the ancient Persian houses served as an example. The principles that governed the planning of both Arab and Moorish houses were derived from classic

Right: *The Joret family furnished the courtyards in the traditional manner, with woven rugs and numerous cushions – soft furnishings still widely used in the Arab world.*

Below: *This view and the one opposite show El Bardo exquisitely maintained in the Edwardian era, photographed by Frederick Evans.*

models; a featureless exterior and an eminently "livable" interior marked the ancient house of Pompeii just as they characterise the Moorish houses of Algiers. Such external ornamentation as there is may be concentrated upon the entrance.' A particularly good example was painted by another intrepid traveller of the Edwardian era: Ella du Cane (*see page 11*).

A much plainer and smaller gate in a high wall leads from El Bardo directly into the gardens of an adjacent summer palace, nowadays used for state functions. Part of its gardens can be peered into from a window in the harem quarters – neglected and tumbledown, but showing traces of their elegant past, with a path leading through

a pergola on terraced land, engulfed by the coils of some magnificent old wisterias.

Though El Bardo has clearly suffered years of neglect during the prolonged periods of strife through the latter half of the twentieth century, a programme of restoration is again underway. The house is now a state museum (the Musée National de Préhistoire et d'Ethnographie du Bardo), displaying archaeological artefacts of the prehistoric and Neolithic periods found in the region, as well as interesting fabrics, pottery, metalwork, jewellery and other crafts. Further rooms are furnished in traditional Moorish style to recreate the ambience of a harem's quarters, displaying a part of the rich legacy of the Joret family.

Above: *The old tiled stairway, with risers picked out in patterned tiles, leads from the carriage drive to the Harem Court, whose entrance is guarded by the 'hand of Fatima'.*

Left: *The columned archway leads into a small loggia and the door to the former quarters of the 'favourite' in the harem. Strelitzias and papyrus add greenery.*

EMERALD PARK, MUSTAPHA SUPÉRIEUR

By the last quarter of the nineteenth century, it felt as though something was missing from the lives of the burgeoning British community in Algiers, settled in considerable splendour on the green and airy heights of Mustapha Supérieur, at some distance from the bustling city. The expatriates had their cool, white villas, their subtropical gardens, their doctors, their dentists, their bank and, since 1870, their own Anglican church by the Porte d'Isly, consecrated on 1 January 1871. They even had, thanks to the French, the tree-lined boulevards of the Jardin d'Essai, a magnificent botanical garden, to stroll in beside the sea at Mustapha Inférieur. But what was needed most of all to make the British feel at home was their own club.

So when the substantial villa of the baron de Royer – ideally located in the heart of Mustapha Supérieur – came up for sale in the late 1880s, a number of members of the British community pooled their resources and formed a limited company to buy it. Thus the English Club was born. Set on a magnificent sloping site, facing north-east with scenic views of the seaport and the white city of Algiers 3 miles distant, the club had sufficient grounds to accommodate two tennis lawns amid the lushness of its palm trees and bougainvilleas; it also administered a nine-hole golf club a twenty-minute walk away, in the Commune of Birmandreïs, which still has an active membership today.

Baron de Royer's former villa, an interesting hybrid of Classical French and neo-Moorish architecture, at once became the focus of gently civilised entertainments throughout the winter season (the club was only open from November to May of each year). These included regular dinners and dances, recitals and the occasional amateur-dramatic performance. British and American visitors could obtain membership for a season, a quarter, a month, or even just a week (subject, of course, to being proposed by two existing members), thereby gaining an essential facility for networking with others of their social class. It was also most conveniently situated a short walk from another favoured venue – the luxurious St George Hotel.

Above: *Baron de Royer's villa became the English Club in the late 1880s. It is shown here among Phoenix and Livistonia palms and squat cycads.*

Left: *The view along the herbaceous border below the balustraded terrace focuses on a tree-framed neighbouring villa, built on higher ground. Many beautiful trees enhance the locality.*

But the English Club's role as a social hub for the British enclave lasted for little more than a generation. Following the death of Alex Macleay, its driving force and co-founder, the club returned to private French ownership for the first six decades of the twentieth century, until Algeria gained its independence.

In 1963, the villa was bought by the British government, since which time it has been the official residence of the British Ambassador to Algiers. Thus, rather neatly, the wheel has turned full circle and Emerald Park (as it has long been known) has been restored to its late-nineteenth-century role as a venue for English-hosted dinners and receptions, functions to which it is admirably suited with its broad terraces and bowling-green lawn.

The villa sits within a 2½-acre plot surrounded by mature palm trees, an ancient rubber tree of great girth, and jacarandas that scatter their pale-violet confetti throughout the spring before their leaves emerge. It is cradled by one of the many meanders of the avenue des Glycines, which weaves a slender ascent between dozens of handsome villas of the belle époque (though today they are all shrouded from view by high walls).

Emerald Park is a rare survivor in modern Algiers, having retained much of its colonial and, yes, clubby atmosphere. The lawn terrace, so admirably suited to games of croquet or the erection of a marquee, is hemmed in by bright flower borders of irises, marguerites, hollyhocks, larkspurs, coreopsis, canna lilies and chrysanthemums. On a lower level, a pretty pavilion in the Moorish style (which serves as a changing room for the swimming pool) looks on to a tennis court whose fencing is swathed in vines, sweet peas and roses. There is an attractive cast-iron greenhouse of French early-twentieth-century design to one side, and at the other end lies a productive potager. One of the most curious aspects of these historic gardens is a separate patch of lawn enclosed by a low wall, where a breeding colony of tortoises resides throughout the year, munching salads and greens left over from the kitchen and, as an occasional treat, hibiscus flowers and foliage.

These gentle scenes may not last much longer, however, as greater demand continues to be made on the land surrounding historic properties that are now part of the bustling city. It would be a great shame if the atmospheric setting for this villa and its magnificent trees, so much a part of Algiers' heritage, was allowed to disappear.

Right: *A corner of the potager of Emerald Park, overlooked by a handsome neighbouring villa on the Chemin des Glycines, a long and winding route up the hillside.*

Below: *Bird-of-paradise flowers (*Strelitzia reginae*) and hollyhocks flourish.*

Campagne Montfeld, Mustapha Supérieur

In 1854, the first Tasmanian blue gum trees, *Eucalyptus globulus*, were introduced to the soils of Algeria and widely welcomed for their 'peculiar power of absorbing miasma'. Planted into swampy ground, a forest of the fast-growing blue gum could rapidly transform unworkable land into useful plots by drying it out. At the same time, there was much interest in the blue gum's aromatic foliage, whose volatile oils have almost magical decongestant and anti-bacterial qualities.

One man who had a particular interest in such things was Eugène Bodichon (1810–85), a tall, dark and charismatic French doctor resident in Algiers, with whom the British painter Barbara Leigh Smith (1827–91) had fallen in love during her first visit to Algiers in the winter of 1856. After they were married in 1857, for the next twenty years Barbara Leigh Smith Bodichon spent most winters in Algiers, and in 1859 she bought a residence for them both, high on the hill of Mustapha Supérieur, with 12 acres of land and views over sloping fields of asphodel to the distant white city and the sea. They renamed their old Ottoman villa Campagne du Pavillon, after the house in Brittany where Eugène Bodichon had spent his childhood.

Mme Bodichon also succeeded in persuading her sister Anne (known as Nannie) to acquire, in the autumn of 1866, the adjacent property, another old villa which had been extended between 1853 and 1863, set in 5 acres of grounds. According to the sales contract, it consisted of 'a large dwelling house, built with a ground floor, a first floor, and outbuildings, which is reached by a tree-lined lane, two other small, low houses with tiled roofs, along with grounds in the form of a garden, an orchard, etc'. Anne Leigh Smith's property, for which she paid 30,000 francs, became known as Campagne Montfeld (*campagne*, in Algerian property terms, meaning an estate, and Montfeld being a corruption of Mountfield, the name of a Leigh Smith family property in Sussex).

When Barbara Bodichon wintered with her husband at Campagne du Pavillon, her sister resided next door with her partner, Isabella Blythe.

Above: *Cycads and oleanders on the terrace. Montfeld is one of the loveliest and best preserved of the old Algerian villas. A swimming pool was added to the terrace in the 1970s.*

Right above: *Detail of traditional pictorial tilework in the gardens.*

Right below: *Carved columns in the fully enclosed entrance courtyard, which has a fountain at its centre in the time-honoured manner.*

Mme Bodichon was a close friend of many artists and writers including George Eliot, Marianne North and Gertrude Jekyll. She brought Miss Jekyll back to Algiers with her in November 1873 and they spent the winter there, venturing into the nearby countryside, painting the unusual flora and landscapes. Miss Jekyll's sketchbook of the trip reveals rocky landscapes of aloes and dwarf irises, a lane bordered by huge opuntias, and a house swathed in crimson bougainvillea. What she does not seem to have painted, tactfully, are the grounds of the two sisters' closely neighbouring homes, which by that stage must have been becoming engulfed by Dr Bodichon's pet interest: his eucalyptus trees, planted in great quantity since 1864.

Nannie Leigh Smith, who had never enjoyed a good relationship with her brother-in-law, implored her sister to make him cut down the fast-growing trees, which, at just a few years old, were rapidly starting to block her views of the Bay of Algiers from the Villa Montfeld. The trees remained, but by the time of Eugène Bodichon's death in Algiers in 1885, North Africa had long since lost its appeal for both Barbara

Bodichon and Nannie Leigh Smith (Barbara's poor health prevented her from travelling there after 1877). Montfeld was let to tenants, though Nannie Leigh Smith maintained ownership of it until March 1909.

It was probably in the 1880s that Benjamin Bucknall was engaged to enlarge and carefully upgrade the house, retaining all its Ottoman features and turning it into one of the most admired houses in Algiers. Both inside and out, the property is unusually rich in colourful tiles, salvaged from countless old houses of Algiers then being demolished.

Beside the Montfeld villa, the flower gardens occupy a sheltered spot on terraced ground where a formal area of raised beds, probably dating from Victorian times, is devoted to cut flowers: larkspurs, coreopsis, carnations, sweet williams and assorted roses. There is also a charming loggia, decorated with old tiles. A path leads from it back to the house via a leafy arbour engulfed by a huge wisteria.

Today, both Montfeld and Pavillon form a substantial part of the large American Embassy complex, Montfeld being the residence of the US Ambassador to Algiers, while Pavillon is now the chancery for the US Consulate. There are beautiful trees everywhere; an avenue of lofty palms lines the drive up to Montfeld, and huge holm oaks, dark cypresses and ancient pines dot the sloping lawns, masking the boundaries of the park.

Above: *Brilliant yellow coreopsis, carnations, roses and larkspurs are among the jolly flowers in the cutting garden. Part of Montfeld's huge wisteria can be seen in the top-left corner.*

Left: *Shade is provided by evergreen oaks and large oleanders, while assorted pots nurture pink pelargoniums. Beyond the gates, further gardens descend the hillside.*

DAR EL OUARD, EL-BIAR

John Reynell Morell's 1854 survey of Algeria observed that on the outskirts of Algiers, 'pretty villas … suspended over abrupt precipices, look like pictures hanging on a wall'. One such pictorial example is Dar El Ouard (the House of the Roses), the fine residence of the Spanish Ambassador to Algiers, a typical white Moorish villa tucked into the hillside, with marvellous sea views from its rocky eyrie high up on the cliffs of El-Biar.

As with so many other properties in the area, this old Ottoman villa, also known as the Spanish Residence, was updated and extended carefully in the nineteenth century and had a succession of British owners, until a French family took it over in 1937. The 5-acre estate was divided in half in 1962, whereupon the Spanish government bought the house and its gardens, while the rest of the estate subsequently became Algerian nationalised property and is now leased to the Turkish Embassy.

Whether you enter the gardens directly from the house or a gateway to one side, it becomes immediately apparent how very steep this site is, necessitating its formal terraces to be long and narrow, following the contour of the hill. While there is a typical Moorish courtyard with arcaded loggia and central fountain at the southern end, the terrace running along the foot of the seaward elevation of the house suggests a

formal layout of the Victorian era, with a lozenge-shaped parterre of low, neatly clipped rosemary hedging, infilled with seasonal flowers – zinnias, antirrhinums and nicotianas – tall *Livistonia chinensis* palm trees, and a *Cycas revoluta* of very great age.

A series of steps and sloping paths drop down from the upper terrace into gardens which are among the most beautifully planted and maintained of any in the region. The beds are colourful, with pink verbenas, blue anchusa, lovely drifts of blue and white agapanthus and seas of iris. Shady areas under the trees are lit up by aubergine-and-white wands of *Acanthus mollis*, a handsome opportunist that readily colonises any spare piece of ground in the neighbourhood. One of the features of these gardens is the great variety of little seats, set among the flowers at convenient points along the garden's many paths. All of them are in the local traditional style, boxy and simple in structure, but prettified by having been covered with faïence tiles (*see page 11*).

These gardens also contain some fine specimen trees. The jacarandas

Above left: *The villa glimpsed through trailing tresses of* Livistonia chinensis *palms and a* Magnolia grandiflora. *The flower gardens are filled with pink verbenas, silver santolina and marguerites, contained in a series of terraced beds enclosed by low retaining walls.*

Above right: *Violet-blue jacaranda beyond magenta bougainvillea.*

Right: *Villa Dar El Ouard, with its main terrace enlivened by orange lantanas.*

tower over neighbouring rooftops and frame views of the busy port, spreading clouds of pale violet among the big fans of stately palms. Above the residence's own flat roof, the gardens continue uphill on a very steep ascent past a huge old water cistern (now converted into a deep and sheer-sided swimming pool). And then, quite unexpectedly, tucked away between an old plantation of slender cypress trees, you come across a little cactus garden, named in honour of the late Père Duran Farell, a prominent Spanish industrialist. A keen amateur botanist, he loved Algeria, its deserts and desert flora, and is in turn still remembered affectionately by its people.

The villas and gardens of Algiers all seem to hold secrets and hidden stories, and the Spanish Residence is no exception: it is believed to have been here that General Eisenhower was secretly billeted for a while during the North African campaign of the Second World War. His room – simple, rather dark and facing out to sea – opens directly on to the terrace, and beside it is a windowless old-fashioned en suite bathroom, a convenience that is thought to have been made specially for his visit and cut into the bedrock of the hill. In the early days of 1944, Lady Diana

Cooper, disillusioned with the Villa Oued-El-Kalaï nearby (*see page 14*), wrote: 'General Eisenhower ... has a fine house which he has vacated today, ... We might, with pull, get it.' They did not. But, as it turned out, the Coopers – or at any rate, Lady Diana – came to love their own property after seeing the gardens burst into flower with the coming of the spring.

In the early 1990s the Spanish government decided it needed further housing on its premises for the Embassy staff and so it employed one of Spain's most celebrated modern architects, Alberto Campo Baeza, to design four houses within the compound. Situated on the left-hand side of the long and winding driveway known as the Avenue Dar El Ouard, Campo Baeza's new houses are striking for the way that, though they are clearly of contemporary design, they also blend in perfectly with the North African vernacular, having few (and small) windows facing outwards into the street, set into sheer, whitewashed walls. As with the Ambassador's ancient residence, the steep gradient means that only the upper two storeys are seen from the street, while the reception rooms, courtyards and gardens are at a lower level, discreetly concealed and facing out towards the bay. Sleeping quarters are confined to the top storeys but, also in the time-honoured way, the houses' flat roofs are also rooftop terraces with marvellous views of the scenic bay of Algiers.

Left: The gardener brings more plants. Carnations and lantanas help to keep the garden colourful.

Below: Potted aloes add spiky decoration to the slender terrace running along the base of the house. Through the treetops, Dar El Ouard enjoys extensive views from its steep hillside perch.

DJENAN-ALI-RAÏS, EL-BIAR

On the bright spring morning of Sunday 21 March 1909, the village square of El-Biar saw a dignified gathering of the members of *Le Comité du Vieil Alger*, the Old Algiers Club, preparing for a rather special outing. Once assembled, they commenced a pleasant stroll down the lane of Ben-Aknoun to the great horseshoe-arched gateway of Djenan-Ali-Raïs. This was a private villa to which invitations were eagerly sought, for it was not only one of the most ancient of the Ottoman properties of Algiers, but also one of the most scrupulously preserved, and situated in a landscape setting of unparalleled beauty, even by the more spacious standards of a hundred years ago.

Algiers and its scenic environs had seen rapid development since French colonisation in 1830, and much of it had been regrettably destructive. By 1881, Alexander Knox observed that the French had thoughtlessly destroyed 'well nigh all the old buildings which might recall the vanished greatness of the place'. By 1905, an Algerian-born

French academic, Henri Klein (1864–1939), had grown desperate, and collected together like-minded people to form *Le Comité du Vieil Alger*. Rather like the early National Trust in England, its aim was to raise awareness of Algiers' remaining treasures and encourage the preservation of imperilled monuments. Djenan-Ali-Raïs, they felt, was exemplary: 'such a contrast to the many nearby villas that one sees throughout the suburbs of our towns, once beautiful, now ugly, and hideously changed, having fallen into the hands of philistines'. Djenan-Ali-Raïs had been a fortunate survivor, painstakingly restored in the 1880s by the English architect Benjamin Bucknall and kept in the hands of successive careful owners.

Above: *The view from the gallery: the court of the harem, glimpsed through an attractive carved balustrade. Compare this with the 100-year-old view on page 49, when plants covered the villa.*

Right: *An Edwardian photograph of the Harem Court, richly furnished with plants. Note the fabric awning that could be pulled out to provide more shade.*

Immediately on entering the park, the *Comité* members were struck by the abundance of huge pine trees, populated with nesting songbirds in great variety whose choruses rang out; they admired its plantation of bamboos, forming a veritable jungle in one of the gulleys washed by an underground stream. A crystal-clear spring-fed lake plunging to a depth of 40 feet covered 2½ acres of ground; its surface mirrored the acrobatics of migrating swallows.

Then there were crowds of date palms and the 5,000 fruit trees of the orchards: oranges, lemons and mandarins spangled with glistening fruits and perfuming the air with their white, waxy-petalled flowers; the garden paths and carriage drive were lined with avenues of cypress, palms and eucalyptus. 'Certainly, the corsaires knew how to create suitable backdrops for their pleasures and dreams!' Klein wrote afterwards.

Unlike many of the older properties, whose origins are obscure, the history of Djenan-Ali-Raïs is well documented. It had been inhabited by two famous sixteenth-century Barbary corsairs – Sala Raïs, who captured Bougie, in eastern Kabylia, from the Spanish and who took over the throne of Muley bon Azau at Fez; and Ali El Euldj Fortas Raïs, a Sicilian captive turned Muslim who distinguished himself at the Siege of Malta in 1565 and at the Battle of Lepanto in 1571. The villa takes its name from the latter ruler and was owned by various aristocratic families of Algeria; in the nineteenth century, it passed to the Bach-Aga Ben Ali Cherif, of Chellata (in Kabylia, east of Algiers). Thereafter, it became the residence of Alex D. Macleay, one of the pillars of the late-nineteenth-century English-speaking community in Algiers, who was the founder and president of the English Club (*see page 32*). During his occupation, Djenan-Ali-Raïs was locally known as the Villa Macleay and it was at this time, in the 1880s, that Benjamin Bucknall carefully updated the comforts of the villa while restoring and conserving its pure Ottoman features.

Above: The outer, entrance courtyard. The gateway in the wide arch at the opposite end led to the stables. A 'skiffa', or reception lobby, can be seen in both pictures.

Right: The view back across the entrance courtyard. These two Edwardian photographs reveal the environs of the house as they had been in the time of the vicomte de Vercelli Ranzy.

The villa was built in typical Moorish form: a hierarchy of inner and outer courtyards, carved marble columns supporting horseshoe-shaped arcades, and, of course, twinkling fountains. 'The first time that I went there,' recalled Klein, 'the chords of an oriental melody vibrated in the fresh air mixed with the scents of the garden. It was almost as if the very soul of the ancient domain was exhaled in this poetic chant.'

The outer courtyard, reached via the carriage drive, led past a plant-filled arcade against a high wall towards the opposite gateway to the stables. A door in the high wall led into the court of the harem, with its octagonal marble fountain and attractive arcaded loggia, with a gallery looking over from the storey above. Beams stretched across the court-yard enabled climbing plants to provide shade from the summer's heat, and colourful majolica tiles decorated window and door frames. Opposite, on the south side, were the guard's room and an under-ground passage, which, it is said, stretched all the way to the Algiers *kasbah*, and which also, more gruesomely, was at some stage discovered to contain chains and skeletons.

Left: The Harem Court today, without the plants and awnings that were enjoyed by the villa's Victorian and Edwardian inhabitants, but revealing a beautifully preserved structure.

Above: An Edwardian photograph taken from the arcaded gallery. Note the abundance of mighty trees that surrounded the villa a century ago, when its park was greatly admired.

In sharp contrast, the rest of the villa revealed delightful confections of pillared interior rooms, featuring fountains and gentle light filtered through central domes above richly carved ceilings. 'The upper part is an absolute delight,' wrote Klein, 'with sitting rooms, galleries and Moorish courtyards equipped with wall hangings copied from the Alhambra, China ornaments from Delft, Sicily and Spain. Wood carvings, copper fretwork, silk hangings, encrusted furniture, and rare plants in full bloom in priceless vases.' There was also a marriage cask from Andalucía – a priceless piece of Moorish cabinetwork – and Japanese-style Indian tapestries. These contents were all part of the collections of the vicomte de Vercelli Ranzy, who acquired the property from Alex Macleay's widow in the early twentieth century, and who hosted the visit of the Old Algiers Club.

It is fascinating to compare *Country Life*'s Edwardian photographs of Djenan-Ali-Raïs, taken during de Vercelli Ranzy's tenure, with the villa as it is today, for there has been little change, except that the courtyards are not throttled by climbing and clinging plants as they were a hundred years ago.

Today, Djenan-Ali-Raïs is pristinely maintained as the residence of the Japanese Ambassador to Algiers, within reduced, though still substantial, gardens attached to a larger estate.

Miss Bart, glowing with the haste of a
precipitate descent upon the train, headed a
group composed of the Dorsets, young
Silverton and Lord Hubert Dacey, who had
barely time to spring into the carriage ...
before the whistle of departure sounded.
The party, it appeared, were hastening to
Nice in response to a sudden summons
to dine with the Duchess of Beltshire and to
see a water-fête in the bay ...

Edith Wharton, *The House of Mirth*

France

'Fortune's Yellow' roses smother a wall on the west side at Lou Sueil, with
views across to the old village of Èze on the adjacent hilltop.

SAINTE-CLAIRE
LE CHÂTEAU, HYÈRES

Made rich over many centuries by its salt pans, its safe naval anchorages and, inland, a cork industry from forests of *Quercus suber* in the Maures mountains, Hyères became a fashionable resort for consumptives after the end of the Napoleonic Wars, though it was never as popular with the British as Menton, way over to the east. Yet, by the early twentieth century, Hyères was like Margate or Biarritz in the early twenty-first: it had seen better days. Lying on the far western fringes of the Riviera, it became a place for more adventurous *hivernants* than would be found at Nice or Monte Carlo, and was patronised by far fewer visitors, though a handful of wealthy Russians could still be seen stalking its casino each winter.

In the 1920s, Hyères reinvented itself as a golfing resort with a luxurious hotel right beside the links course. 'There is no tiresome long drive or walk before one begins to play,' observed one travel writer, while an alluring advertising poster depicted Hyères as an intriguing old town beyond the golfers in the foreground, its little buildings clustered round a steep hill crowned by mysterious towers and ramparts.

And that is the most intriguing part of it for us, for that hilltop was by that time the Riviera domain of the American novelist Edith Wharton, who had been gardening there since the end of the First World War. She had taken a lease on the property, known as Sainte-Claire le Château, from Alfred Pechiney, a wealthy industrialist; and in 1927, she bought it outright from him, with more land into the bargain.

Above: *Photographed in the mid-1920s, the main terrace in Edith Wharton's day, with 'cartwheel' pruned plane trees and a southerly aspect overlooking Hyères.*

Left: *The front courtyard. The huge magenta-flowered Judas tree,* Cercis siliquastrum, *used to dominate the entrance, though this venerable specimen has long since disappeared.*

Occupying part of the site of an ancient fortress dating back to before Roman times, with strategic views of the coastal plain, Edith Wharton's elegant house had been a convent of the Order of Poor Clares, which did good works in the town. In the middle of the nineteenth century, it was acquired and extensively refurbished by Olivier Voutier, the former naval ensign who became famous for his discovery of the *Venus de Milo* in Greece, in 1820 (his tomb is in the grounds). A near neighbour had been Robert Louis Stevenson, who had settled in Hyères in 1882 at Le Chalet de la Solitude, a faux-Swiss folly close to Sainte-Claire. With such historical and literary associations attached to this little hill, it is easy to see why the author of *The Age of Innocence* and *The House of Mirth* decided to put her roots down here.

When Wharton bought the property from Pechiney, her land reached over all sides of the 600-foot hill with its encircling line of towers and ramparts. Consequently, she was able to indulge her passion for plants by venturing higher and higher up the hillside to make new areas of garden: blasting out the rock here, and there using the smashed stones to build retaining walls for the terraces. She must have been less than popular with the locals, however, when her acquisition of the north face of the hill prompted her to close off a rough track through the olives; until then, anybody could stroll among sheets of wild anemones,

orchids, violets and periwinkles – a romantic route in springtime up to the castellated round tower.

But that was up above and around about; down below, the approach drive was cheerfully and fragrantly lined with purple irises in spring, complementing the château terrace's grey buttresses, turned 'blue with kennedya' (now known as *Hardenbergia violacea*). That long main terrace, spanning out alongside the house and reached via a trellised gate overhung with anemone roses, was dignified by two plane trees with flat canopies pruned into rough cartwheels, creating shady umbrellas for anyone who might wish to sit under them in the summer. From there, the gardens continued upwards and eastwards, with much use made of vertical cypress trees, so loved by Mrs Wharton, whose high regard for Italian villa gardens had led her to write a book about them in 1904. The most striking trees, which predated Mrs Wharton's arrival, included a magnificent Judas tree (*Cercis siliquastrum*) at the centre of the gravelled entrance courtyard, and a huge carob under which were planted swathes of blue violas.

Right: *Today, the slender cypress trees that Edith Wharton planted in quantity dominate the garden and plunge much of it into shade, making it difficult for other plants to thrive.*

Below: *The terrace, set strategically high on the hill, overlooks the old church of Hyères, with the Maures mountains beyond. In Mrs Wharton's day, the hills were undeveloped.*

In spring, the garden's main season, you might clamber up rustic stone steps and shuffle along little paths following the contours of the hill, past crimson cherries, magenta blossoms of Judas trees, drifts of pale-blue iris and, creeping among the rocks, the yellow-centred blue daisies of *Felicia amelloides*. Wharton's 'Japanese' garden was a very formal, levelled terrace, with pink- and white-blossomed cherry trees lining a lawned walk, either side of which were flowerbeds in two long, broad bands filled with freesias. The scent in this garden must have been glorious at its early-spring flowering time. Another terrace was devoted to an avenue of standard mandarin trees, under which were more yellow freesias, with the views to the south framed by a hedge of cypress arches.

Where the terrain was tricky and steep, olives and agaves were allowed to grow wild among the boulders, enlivened by orange freesias, African daisies, blue anemones, periwinkles and violets. One particularly rocky area was devoted to a huge collection of succulents and cacti, said to be more complete than even the renowned collection of the Prince of Monaco. Nearby, a lawned walk focusing on the distant round tower was enriched by a row of blue violas and the delicate pink flowers of *Raphiolepis indica*, the 'Indian hawthorn' whose flowers resemble plum blossom.

Edith Wharton frequently described her Riviera life, particularly in letters to friends and relations. The garden was in its infancy when she wrote to Beatrix Farrand in March 1920: 'Ste Claire, of which I send you some quite inadequate photos, is in the hands of masons & diggers of the earth. It is almost impossible to "take," as it's all up & downhill, but these snaps will give you some idea of its militant air, & the way it leans against the old *mur d'enceint*, guarded by its 2 towers. Mr. Nabormand, the "rosièriste" of Golfe Juan, came to see us (or rather *it*) the other day, & was in raptures at my series of terraces, & at the opportunity for growing camellias & gardenias, besides all the roses that ever *were*. Here, at present, the whole country is gushing with roses – Banksia, Laevigata & hybrid teas – which, after one outburst in Dec., & then a gentle steady flowering all winter, have now cast aside all restraint, & are smothering walls, house fronts & balconies in white & crimson & golden breakers of bloom.'

The next winter, she wrote to her sister-in-law, Mary Cadwalader Jones, of '... the happiest Xmas I have spent in many a long year. I can wish no old woman of my age a better one! The little house is delicious, so friendly & comfortable, & full of sun & air; but what overwhelms us all – though we thought we knew it – is the endless beauty of the view, or rather the views ...' The 'divinest Riviera weather' brought the household out to have coffee on the terrace after luncheon, but the euphoria of winter sunshine was soon to be cruelly demolished by a sudden hard frost.

'My terraces were just beginning to be full of bursting sprouting things, & it was really sickening to see the black crepy rags which, a few

hours before, were heliotropes, "anthemises", tradescantia, plumbago, arums, geraniums – all the stock-in-trade of a Riviera garden – dangling woefully from the denuded terraces,' Wharton confessed to Mary Cadwalader Jones. 'The orange trees were severely frozen, & some of the old ones may be lost; & even my splendid old caroube trees, which had put on their glorious dense shining foliage in October, are all frizzled & brown. Eucalyptus & pepper-trees are shrivelled up, & the huge prickly pears that were the pride of the place are falling apart like paper flowers the day after a procession.'

Locals say that a truly destructive winter occurs only every twenty years or so, but this setback right at the start of Wharton's Riviera gardening career did not deter her, as the photographs of 1928 testify. On that occasion, Euan Cox admired the plant collections and rarities: 'Every few yards one comes across some plant which is rarely seen on the Riviera, for Mrs Wharton is not satisfied with growing the ordinary routine herbaceous plants or shrubs, and in most cases her experiments are very successful. One example may be given in the illustration of *Acacia catheriana*, one of the rarest of the late-flowering mimosas.'

Sit on Edith Wharton's broad stone terrace today and you still get a marvellous bird's-eye view over the handsome pantiled roofs of old Hyères and the distant age-worn granite undulations of the Maures mountains, though a glance at the early photographs reveals how very much of the area has been built over, with villas crowding the hills and high-rise developments on the edge of town. Her garden has changed, too, and is really only Edith Wharton's in name. The cypress trees she planted with abandon have grown so large that practically nothing will grow in their shadow; the lawns are gone, the gardens drastically reduced in size, interest and ambition. Southwards, in the misty distance, there is still the calm expanse of the sea, rolling up to the salt marshes beyond the ancient town. Even so, Mrs Wharton would not recognise the creatures of the air rising out of those marshes now, since substantial areas have been drained and hard-surfaced for the jets taking off from Toulon-Hyères airport. In spite of all this, Hyères remains a handsome, charming town, which, like an ageing French film star, has managed to hold on to much of its allure.

Above right: Edith Wharton's successful novels paid for new garden features such as this smart pergola and stone retaining wall, clearly recent acquisitions at the time of this photograph.

Left: The rock garden, blasted out of a sheer precipice, contained a remarkable and unparalleled collection of succulents. A rare Tetrapanax papyrifer *brightens the left corner.*

LOU SUEIL, ÈZE

The villa Lou Sueil (meaning the hearth, or threshold, in local vernacular) epitomised the elegant and carefree Riviera lifestyle of the inter-war years. Edith Wharton often travelled from Hyères to inspect the gardens and Winston Churchill frequently painted them. Over luncheon Charlie Chaplin once regaled the party with hilarious anecdotes of his terrifying first experience of hunting, following the Duke of Westminster's hounds, and the handsome Maharajah of Kapurthala always brought with him boxes of mangoes fresh from his Indian orchards. On one New Year's Eve, the aged Duke of Connaught, Queen Victoria's third son, dozed peacefully through a concert put on for him there by the Monte Carlo Quartet, and in 1925, Lord Curzon arrived with trunks of files and manuscripts so that he could spend a quiet fortnight editing his copious Indian memoirs, spreading out his papers over several Chippendale tables.

At Lou Sueil, picnics were packed for days out plant-hunting in the nearby hills with Lawrence Johnston and Norah Lindsay, and Lord Berners' Rolls-Royce (complete with a harmonium for impromptu compositions) purred down the long driveway, with delicate butterflies pinned to the interior lining.

It was during the 'lovely months of winter sunshine' from 1922 to 1938 that the châtelaine of Lou Sueil, Consuelo Vanderbilt Balsan (1877–1964), an American heiress and a former Duchess of Marlborough, hosted many convivial events to which invitations were eagerly accepted. They included lively lunch parties that she seemed to regret had to be 'limited to twenty, at two tables of ten', after which came obligatory tours of the garden. There was a short route for the elderly and infirm, 'with a more extended tour for the hale and hearty'. What could they expect to see?

For one thing, the panoramas were unrivalled anywhere on the Riviera. Looking westwards, beyond the immediate formality of the Italian garden, the ancient hilltop village of Èze, 'hanging on by all fingers and toes to the steep rocks', could be viewed across a chasm, prettily framed by the spires of Lou Sueil's slender cypress trees. Southwards, the land dropped away steeply through olive groves and pine-clad rocks, down to the seaside at Èze-sur-Mer, with the lovely peninsula of Cap Ferrat and its sailboats spread out to the south-west. Eastwards lay Cap d'Ail and Monaco, and all around behind the protective stony summits of the Alpes-Maritimes.

Garden visitors, however, might almost be forgiven for hardly noticing the views, for close at hand was certainly one of the loveliest gardens of the inter-war period. Consuelo Balsan compared her grounds to the hanging gardens of Babylon: 'hung in mid-air and unless terraced on stone walls, [it] would have crumbled down the steep mountainside'. The summit of the hill had been levelled out for the villa and its formal gardens, but the steep slopes around it were managed with stone retaining walls. Flights of steps were expertly made with just the right

The Balsans' new villa in the 1920s, viewed from the south-east, where the sloping ground was planted with specimen aloes, leading to more relaxed flower gardens downhill.

Above: *The exquisite wrought-iron gateway from the cloister.*

Right: *Looking from the triple-arched summerhouse to the parterre garden of low hedges and coloured gravels, surrounded by cypress trees.*

amount of rough-hewn rusticity, and paths of finely crushed gravel snaked between the almond and olive trees among massed plantings of spring bulbs.

The architect of the villa and its adjacent formal gardens was Achille Duchêne (1866–1947), a fashionable choice already familiar to Consuelo, not least because he had designed Sunderland House in Mayfair for her first husband, the Duke of Marlborough, at the turn of the century. Achille and his father, Henri, both distinguished landscape architects, were famed in France for their Classical restoration of some of the great formal gardens, including those of Château Vaux-le-Vicomte and Château de Courances, and had created others in the eighteenth-century style.

At Lou Sueil, Duchêne was presented with a very different sort of challenge: to leave behind the formal French style that had been his trademark prior to the First World War. Here he was to build a comfortable villa home, modelled on the Cistercian simplicity of Le

Thoronet, an eleventh-century Provençal convent. Completed in 1922, it was a triumph, fashioned out of the pale-grey local stone quarried at La Turbie, with the door and window arches made in the hard cream limestone of Avignon. Amazingly, this fabulous house took barely a year to build. During that time, local farmers became used to the sight of six burly brothers, all of them stonemasons, walking over the mountains from Italy every Monday and making a return march at the end of each week to spend Sunday with their wives.

Within the villa complex, the brothers built a remarkable cloister, with stout columns and vaulted roofs in the same cream-coloured stone that the Romans had quarried to build the Pont du Gard. Following monastic precedent, the cloister's garden was serenely formal, with herringbone-patterned brick paths criss-crossing a four-square design of tiny lawns edged by low box hedges, the composition focusing on a central font planted with seasonal flowers.

Immediately west of the villa and its cloister, Duchêne made a formal parterre, known as the Italian garden, fashioned in low box hedging and infilled with contrastingly coloured gravels of brick-red and cream. Where its central paths crossed over, the focus was on a magnificent, rose-red marble trough, out of which arose a basin carved from a single piece of marble, brought from a monastery in the Pyrenees. Around the garden's edge, slender cypress trees stood erect beside rows of potted carnations; stone troughs were planted with vermilion cinerarias, echoing the darker gravel of the parterre and the floor tiles of a small, arch-fronted summerhouse.

But this was the Riviera, and even Duchêne found that rigorous formality could not be maintained for anything but a short sprint. Where the land dropped away steeply beyond the villa, more relaxed and exuberant planting took over. A lawn just below the villa was dedicated to a huge collection of mimosas, perfect specimens in varied sulphur, lemon and orange hues, here and there underplanted with blue carpets of *Anemone blanda*. Further lawns beneath the many old olive trees were brilliant with the colours of thousands of tulips, *Anemone fulgens*, narcissus, pink hyacinths and white crocus. And on the piers of stairways, oil jars were filled with azure clouds of *Agathea coelestis*, the dainty South African daisy we know today as *Felicia amelloides*.

One stairway led down to a magnificent walk proceeding between tall olive trees a-flutter with white fantail doves; beside the path, a long white colonnade was garlanded with the pink clusters of 'American Pillar' roses. The underplanting was a carpet of blue cinerarias and forget-me-nots, outlined by ribbons of nemophila. Further paths scurried through 'brilliant fields of antirrhinum', while sunlit banks were variously bathed in massed irises of mixed pastel hues, or sheets of pot marigolds, or, elsewhere, 'a kaleidoscope of all colours of ranunculus'. 'Fortune's Yellow' roses engulfed a low wall beside an orchard of orange trees on the western side, framing the distant views of old Èze with gold in the springtime.

In her memoirs, Consuelo recalled her Riviera garden with deep affection – and some appreciation of the labours involved in creating it: 'Almond trees bloomed first, in pink and white showers; then came the prunus and the Judas trees with their bronze and scarlet foliage. Every month had its particular mimosa cascading in yellow fragrance. Like those Gothic tapestries strewn with flowers, our gardens represented endless toil. In September, after the first rains that softened the soil, we scattered thousands of bulbs; gardeners followed on their knees with trowels. A happy medley of colours was thus achieved, and the effect looked natural. All these bulbs had to be dug up in May and replanted the following autumn, for the drought and heat of summer would have shrunk and killed them.'

And flowers were not confined to the outdoors. Every room offered the potential for vases artistically filled with sprigs of fragrant blossoms and the silvery leafage of the *maquis*. Consuelo later remembered that 'the house was gay with flowers. The scent of tuberoses, lilac and lilies filled the air. When one entered the cloisters, a succession of flame-coloured azaleas was a lovely sight.' Yet it seems that the sheer exuberance of the planting and its rich use of bulbs, blossoms and choice

Right above: *The formal parterre garden, with box hedging and infills of coloured gravels.*

Right centre: *The driveway through natural pine forest.*

Right below: *A peasant house on the hillside was transformed into a guesthouse and deep-red wallflowers were planted among the olives, providing vivid colour and scent in spring.*

Opposite: *Old Èze looks over land that was levelled to make a sumptuous lawn below the villa.*

flowering shrubs were never allowed to compromise the overall natural beauty of an olive-and-pine-wooded landscape. Very large areas were devoted to gardening of one kind or another; woodland paths around the tennis courts were filled with fragrant shrubs; inaccessible rocky banks supported succulent aloes.

So is Consuelo Vanderbilt Balsan one of the 'forgotten' gardeners in that great age which also nurtured the celebrated Ellen Willmott, Beatrix Farrand, Vita Sackville-West and Norah Lindsay? Certainly, the earlier years of her life do not suggest that horticultural greatness would come later. Who would have thought that this dark-haired beauty, raised in the best salons of New York society, only to be whisked off aged eighteen to the splendours of Blenheim, possessed such a talent for gardening? Her green fingers did not emerge until the difficult decade prior to her marriage to Jacques Balsan in 1920.

After separating from the Duke of Marlborough in 1906, Consuelo lived in London and continued the rounds of house parties and charitable committees, until in 1910 she felt the need to find a weekend retreat within easy reach of the city. Crowhurst Place, a romantic, medieval and Tudor property surrounded by moats on the borders of Surrey and Sussex, provided the answer. Consuelo was able to take over the lease on it from the architect, George Crawley, who had begun making alterations but needed to sell up due to financial difficulties and his wife's failing health. Consuelo in turn engaged Crawley to complete the works, and they quickly refurbished and extended the house. He also laid out a glorious progression of labour-intensive gardens in the Arts and Crafts style that was then being so successfully prescribed by Edwin Lutyens and Gertrude Jekyll. At the end of the war, Consuelo moved to Paris, gave up Crowhurst and leased a villa at Èze-sur-Mer to be near her mother. It lay at the bottom of the very mountainside that she and Jacques Balsan later purchased.

In 1927, it was no less a connoisseur than Euan Cox who revealed the treasures of Lou Sueil to a wider audience, in two articles in *Country Life*. As the magazine's gardens editor, Cox had a keen and informed interest in Mediterranean flora and in the diverse ways that gardens were being made and planted in the fashionable Riviera. He was unequivocal in his praise of Lou Sueil. 'The gardens are magnificent and unique,' he wrote, 'for no others can exist where hillside gardening is carried out on so large a scale; and there seems to be no end to the gardening operations that can be and are being devised.' Though it was only five years old by this stage, he pronounced that 'in a few years' time it will be one of the greatest of the world's gardens'.

In the 1930s the garden was opened to visitors for charity, making as much as 100,000 francs in one winter. But at the end of the decade, with Nazi troops advancing on Paris, the Balsans left France and did not take up residence at Lou Sueil again until after the Second World War. Later, it was bought by Princess Marie Gabrielle of Savoy.

Now, under a different name, the domain of Lou Sueil continues to be one of the key properties of the Riviera, although in private and guarded seclusion.

The dovecote at the end of the long pergola. On the left are 'Paulette' roses rising out of rough grass under a fig tree and beneath the olives on the right swathes of deep-red antirrhinums.

LES COLLETTES, CAGNES-SUR-MER

The origins of the olive tree may be lost in the mists of time – the oldest fossilised leaves of a wild olive tree, found in Greece, have been carbon-dated to *circa* 37,000 BC, while those discovered in France go back a mere 7,000 years – but it is the Phoenicians who are credited with introducing the cultivation of olive trees to France when they founded Marseilles in 600 BC. The mysterious, beneficient olive tree found a sympathetic home in the limestone hills and coastline of Provence and the Alpes-Maritimes. And at Les Collettes, tucked away on those calcareous hills midway between Nice and Antibes, it was the olive trees that bewitched Auguste Renoir (1841–1919) in the twilight years of his productive life, turning the artist unexpectedly into a conservationist.

Renoir became captivated by the light and landscapes of the South of France in the 1880s, when he travelled there with Claude Monet. He

had already been in search of winter sunshine in Algiers, first in early 1881 and again in the spring of 1882. After those two trips, he settled for the nearer shores of southern France instead of those of its aromatic North African colony, a thirty-six-hour sea voyage from Marseilles.

From 1900, Renoir and his wife, Aline, became regular winter visitors to the Côte d'Azur, lured south by the mild climate, which might ease a little the artist's arthritic illness. He had not intended to buy property on the rapidly expanding (and increasingly expensive) Riviera, for they already owned a farmhouse at Essoyes, Aline's home village in southern Champagne. Yet when he was advised in 1907 that the farm of Les Collettes with its ancient olive grove on the hill behind Cagnes was to be sold off and the trees felled, he felt driven to act. The farm's huge and characterful olives, some of which are believed to be between 500 and 1,000 years old, were to be grubbed up and destroyed, and, in a scene suggestive of Marcel Pagnol's *Jean de Florette*, the land was to be cleared to make way for intensive production of carnations for the burgeoning cut-flower market.

Left: *A bust of Claude 'Coco' Renoir, the artist's youngest son, sits on a marble fireplace in the drawing room. The family moved into their new house in 1908.*

Below: *The attractive farmhouse in its grounds provided an inexhaustible subject for Renoir to paint, filling the artist with nostalgia for the old peasant ways.*

Renoir left the little huddle of farm buildings as they were, set into the south-west-facing slope beside the olive grove, but he built a new house complete with a north-facing studio higher up the hill and moved his family – Aline and their two younger sons, Jean (aged thirteen) and Claude (aged five) – there in the autumn of 1908. With its panoramic southerly views taking in Nice and the Baie des Anges, and its west-wards focal point across a little valley to the medieval hill village of Haut-de-Cagnes, Les Collettes captivated and inspired the artist as completely as any of his voluptuous models.

The little rustic farm filled him with nostalgia for the old peasant ways and lifestyle, even then rapidly disappearing. There was the terraced meadow of tall, oaty grasses shimmering gold and silver in the breeze and, of course, the olives, whose shade softens the sunlight but never entirely eliminates it, flickering above great buttressed and petrified roots. He even had a wooden studio constructed among the trees (demolished in the 1950s), hung with cotton fabric at its windows to filter the sunshine. From inside, he observed the fugitive colours and changing light that often caused him frustration: 'The olive tree! What a brute! If you realised how much trouble it has caused me! A tree full of colours. Not great at all. How all those little leaves make me sweat! A gust of wind and my tree's tonality changes. The colour isn't on the leaves, but in the spaces between them.'

It was down to Aline to make a garden, leading away from the south elevation of the house. Roses were planted against its walls, trailing over the archways, and a formal garden was laid out further on, filled with fragrant shrub roses and the latest hybrid teas, with plenty of pink or blush flowers, Renoir's favourites, which feature in many of his paintings. Mme Renoir planted rows of citrus trees – mandarins and oranges – between the roses; there were also spring-flowering irises, autumn-flowering dahlias and fashionable yuccas. Aline explained to the sculptor Auguste Rodin when he visited: 'There are no rare flowers here, but marguerites next to the mimosa. My husband likes common or garden flowers.' The kitchen garden beside the farmhouse was also a hive of productivity, keeping the little 9-acre estate more or less self-sufficient through the year in the time-honoured way.

The idyllic years that produced Renoir's most mellowed work passed rapidly, however. His sons Pierre and Jean Renoir, who had enlisted at the outbreak of the First World War, were both wounded; Aline, exhausted by the war and the consequent travelling to visit her sons in military hospitals, died in 1915, following years of illness caused by diabetes. When the war was over, Jean returned to live with his father at Cagnes, but by then everything was overgrown and desolate.

When Renoir died in 1919, Les Collettes passed to his youngest son, Claude, who continued to live there until 1960, when it was sold to the town of Cagnes-sur-Mer and the general council of the Alpes-Maritimes to create a museum. Here, the remarkable legacy of the artist can be seen, both in the superbly maintained house with its small collection of his works, its studio with paints and brushes seemingly at the ready, and its gardens, with the great olives shimmering beyond.

The ancient, gnarled olive trees, seemingly as old as time, were the principal reason Renoir acquired Les Collettes, so that he could prevent them being felled.

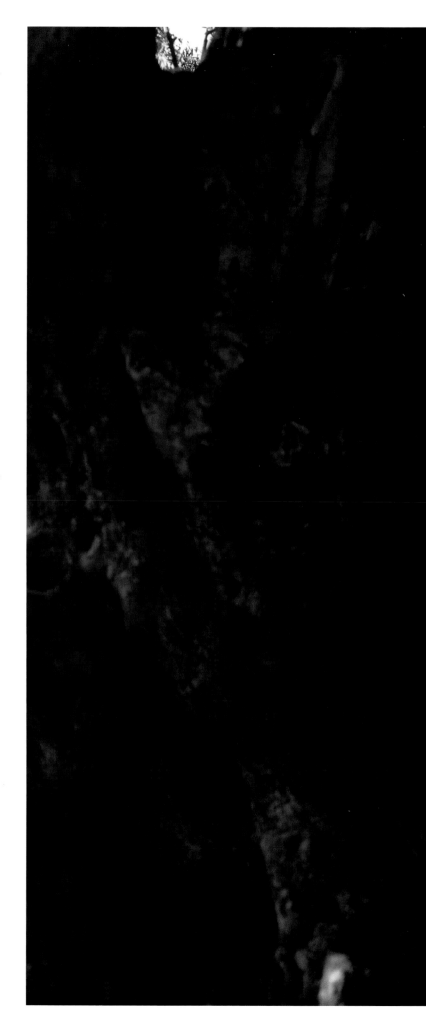

VILLA MARYLAND, SAINT-JEAN-CAP-FERRAT

In many ways the perfect Riviera house, the Villa Maryland enjoyed extensive coverage in *Country Life* when it was first featured in 1910. In fact, the pre-First World War article by H. Avray Tipping is probably the longest single feature on a brand-new property ever to appear in the magazine, extending to ten pages (devoted to the upper gardens) on 3 December, with another nine pages (on the lower gardens and villa) completing the story the following week. The garden was well enough admired by *Country Life* to be featured again in 1926. What was all the fuss about?

Maryland was one of the three great villa-and-garden properties conceived from start to finish by the architect Harold Peto at the dawn of the twentieth century. (The other two were Villas Sylvia (*see page 108*) and Rosemary, also on Cap Ferrat.) Peto designed substantial parts of many other Riviera properties, but these three stand head and shoulders above the rest of his work because he was involved in every aspect of them: creating the villa, its garden, its planting, its ancillary buildings, garden sculptures and the complete house interiors, which he furnished with antiques and specially commissioned masonry brought over from

Italy. The Riviera was fortunate, for here was a fifty-year-old genius architect, a cultured man and keen gardener, who was at the height of his creative powers. The Villa Maryland, in particular, gives us an unadulterated view of the master and his art, his vision of a complete and perfect property.

Crowning one of the many little hills that make up the exclusive Cap Ferrat, Villa Maryland enjoys 360-degree views taking in, to the north across a tree-speckled valley, the Villa Île de France (also known as Villa Ephrussi de Rothschild; *see page 80*) framed by the Alpes-Maritimes; southwards, one's gaze is drawn downhill to the attractive little harbour of Saint-Jean-Cap-Ferrat, with its crowd of sailboats and the wooded finger of Saint-Hospice beyond; while views east and west overlook the beautiful bays of Villefranche and Beaulieu. The plot for Maryland,

Right: *View from the temple, located on the garden's western boundary. It forms the main axis of the upper gardens, leading back to the villa. Arum lilies thrive at the pool's edge.*

Below: *The Villa Maryland, Peto's Riviera masterpiece as it was in 1910, viewed from the sunken garden. The upper floor of the two-storey cloister, on the far right, is at the same level as the villa's ground floor. Much later, the lawn made way for a swimming pool.*

which was originally called St Hiliers, was substantial by Riviera standards, amounting to 4 acres made up of several contiguous pieces of hillside, formerly peasant smallholdings of limited productivity.

Peto's clients were Mr and Mrs Arthur Wilson, members of a family that had acquired enormous wealth in the shipyards of Hull, on Yorkshire's east coast, with the rise of steamship travel in the nineteenth century. The Wilson Line had become the largest privately owned steamship company in the world, and the change of their Riviera property's name from St Hiliers to Maryland was associated with the company's transatlantic trade (though they also owned a steamship called *Maryland*).

So Peto's design for the plot, which has been likened to the layout of a ship, almost seems inevitable. Whether it was a conscious or subconscious decision, Maryland's flower gardens do appear, on plan, to be

Above: The villa and main garden were sited well above the road, as the gradient of the site was so steep. The start of the long, pillared rose pergola of the lower gardens can be seen in the bottom right-hand corner. The quality and quantity of plants is impressive.

Left: The central stairway divides the steeply sloping lower gardens across the lane. Flights of steps run down either side from the belvedere to join the centre stair.

reaching forward like the prow of a mighty liner into the silvery sea of the surrounding landscape. Yet such an analogy is not particularly unusual for gardens made during this great age of Edwardian cruise-ship travel, which saw the building of the superliners *Mauretania* (whose interiors were designed by Harold Peto), *Lusitania* and *Titanic*. Béatrice de Rothschild's Villa Île de France, built shortly after Maryland, is also said to be nautically inspired (even to the point where her garden staff wore sailor suits), while in England at Sedgwick Park, nautical references in its design (in which Peto may have been involved) were carried through to the point where specific areas of the garden were labelled 'The Upper Deck', 'The Quarter Deck', 'The White Sea', and so on.

Maryland is special because of the absolute coherence of its design and, funds being generous, the very high quality of its execution, although there was one flaw to be surmounted. A public right of way, 'an irremovable element that could not be circumvented', ran eastwards up the hill from the main road now known as avenue Denis Séméria; it tiresomely cut the Maryland plot in half just below its highest point.

After considering every option, Peto concluded that the only place to site the villa was at the highest point of the property, just north of the lane but jammed up directly beside it. He judged that since it was a cul-de-sac serving only the Maryland-St Hilier plots and one or two immediate neighbours, it was unlikely to prove troublesome and might even be advantageous for access to the new house. Likewise, access to the lower gardens was achieved by building a little bridge over the lane, linking the villa's terrace to a graceful stairway descending into the lower, south-facing grounds.

Enter the villa from the road and you ascend the stairway of a square, double-height cloister, Peto's clever reworking of the Roman peristyle and the Moorish patios he had admired in southern Spain. Because of the steep gradient, the villa and its main garden were raised some 13 feet above the lane, successfully masking its presence.

Level gardens leading westwards away from the house (at first-floor level, as far as the road was concerned) were divided into lawned and hedged 'rooms'. A gravelled walk along the southern edge proceeded through a tunnel of clipped cypress trees, edged by a cleverly topiarised cypress arcade. This led into a curved pergola and typical Peto 'temple' on the western boundary, with a central gravel path heading back to the house through a series of flower gardens – twenty-eight formal beds, richly and informally planted – among the old olives and neat citrus trees. A large old Roman corn jar marked the central point of this area, surrounded by 'yielding colour schemes perfectly agreeable to the most fastidious taste': they included dwarf mimosas, orange trees, azaleas, silver-leaved westringia, peonies, dicentras and lilies.

The lawns nearer the villa were dotted with old olives; beside the house there were sunny borders filled for winter and spring with wallflowers, cinerarias, nemesias, violas, assorted daisies and aubrieta. To the north was the wild garden, where the distinctive olive trees were garlanded here and there with wisteria and underplanted with seas of irises, narcissi and anemones.

As if all of this was not enough, there was further horticultural splendour to be experienced in the lower gardens, south of the lane. A mighty stairway edged with an avenue of vertical cypresses led down to an Italian fountain with the vista terminating in another temple, which marked the southern boundary. The planting on either side was enlivened with fragrant swathes of lavender, blue-flowered echiums and *Kniphofia caulescens*. Running eastwards below the lane, rendered brick-work piers formed a splendid long pergola engulfed in 'choice roses and other climbers', rising out of further flower borders. Yet the effect was never overdone, and substantial areas of the lower gardens were allowed to be restful and unmanicured, scattered with wild flowers under silvery olives and the refreshing blossoms of plum and almond trees.

Peto's Riviera gardens all reveal how well he manipulated space, not wasting so much as a square yard of land, but bringing it all into the frame of the domain, and never spoiling naturally beautiful areas or sacrificing a fine view. His architectural style – a honed blend of

The view to the temple on the western boundary from halfway along the main axis. The roofline of the neighbouring Villa Les Cèdres can be seen beyond the cypress topiaries and olive trees on the left.

inspirations from the neighbouring Mediterranean lands of Italy (including Ancient Rome), Moorish Spain and North Africa – suited the Côte d'Azur landscape so well that it became the style of choice for those who could afford it. Many imitators came later; one of the most successful was Ferdinand Bac, whose most engaging work is clearly derivative of Peto's.

An interesting twist to the tale of the Villa Maryland is that Peto was simultaneously creating lavish gardens in England for Daisy Brooke, Countess of Warwick, at Easton Lodge in Essex. Daisy was linked to the Tranby Croft affair, a scandal that was nearly the undoing of the socially ambitious Wilsons. At their Yorkshire mansion of Tranby Croft, the Wilsons had hosted, on 8 September 1890, a house party at which the Prince of Wales was present – as was Daisy, who was then his mistress. One member of the party was observed cheating during a game of cards – the then illegal game of baccarat – with the prince playing the part of banker. When the scandal became public it led to a famous lawsuit that held the nation in thrall, not least because the Prince of Wales was made to testify as a witness. It was widely believed that the scandal only came to trial because the beautiful and irre-pressible Daisy (known as the 'babbling Brooke') could not resist broadcasting the private scandal of the cheating guest to her friends. By the time Peto had laid out Daisy's impressive gardens in 1903, she and the prince had long since parted company. But one wonders whether the well-connected architect ever casually mentioned to his Riviera clients that his creative flair was also being bestowed on the gardens of the troublesome countess.

Villa Maryland has fared better than some of the great Riviera proper-ties of the belle époque; little has altered externally and the gardens (certainly until very recently) are not greatly changed from Peto's design. It is still the private playground of a tycoon, though these days the key players at such places are more likely to be leading the field in information technology.

Above: *The upper storey of the cloister, with marble columns garlanded in roses. The lower storey of the cloister contains a stairway leading up to the ground floor of the villa.*

Right: *White arum lilies,* Zantedeschia aethiopica, *in a bog bed next to the pool. The steps lead up to the temple summerhouse on the garden boundary.*

VILLA ÎLE DE FRANCE, CAP FERRAT

After all the effort it took to build the Villa Île de France (later known as Villa Ephrussi de Rothschild) and to create its fabled gardens, it seems remarkable that its maker spent so very little time there. Occupying the narrow isthmus near the northern end of Cap Ferrat, its 18 acres were acquired in 1905 by Baroness Charlotte Béatrice de Rothschild (1864–1934) a third-generation scion of the famous banking family and the wife of banker Maurice Ephrussi.

The house crowns the hilltop so that you can see it clearly from across the bay of Villefranche on the one hand, and that of Beaulieu on the other: a gorgeous pink ice-cream confection nestled into a crowd of mature umbrella pines and palm trees. Likewise, of course, the villa enjoys spectacular views in all directions and the Baroness was fortunate in sealing the deal quickly – just ahead of the Belgian King Leopold II, who coveted it and who had already cannily purchased many other tracts of land on the Cap.

The lawns of the water garden, dotted with palms and stout agaves and surrounding a long canal, make a calm setting. Many thousands of visitors every year are delighted when the fountains dance all day in a succession of whirling patterns in time to jolly Viennese waltzes. Even in midwinter this delightfully frivolous aquatic concert continues and there is still much in bloom, for these gardens were originally made, like all of them prior to the 1930s, to be enjoyed through winter and spring. So winter can still see a few pink roses in bloom; in light shade there will be little button rosettes of sasanqua camellias; and, under the canopies of old olives, careless drifts of pale-blue Algerian iris (*I. unguicularis*) line secret little earthen paths.

Baroness Béatrice was a great art collector and Île de France housed many of her pictures, tapestries and pink and green Sèvres porcelain. Miriam Rothschild described her as 'possessed of the remorseless energy of her gifted uncle Edmond ... beautiful, with white hair at the

The villa sits at the northern end of the site, with lozenge-shaped gardens straddling the hilltop as they extend southwards. The treatment adjacent to the house was strictly formal in the French manner, with an elegant water garden occupying the long main north–south axis. On the terrace beside the villa, immaculate emerald lawns still have a camber towards their edges giving a distinctly cushioned, rich effect. Edged with beds of roses and bedding plants and displaying crest-emblazoned glazed urns, this area and the water garden beyond it are well maintained, preserving as much as is possible the feeling of a lavish, labour-intensive garden of the belle époque. Forty gardeners landscaped the grounds, and the permanent staff was apparently dressed in sailor suits, enhancing the property's faintly nautical inspiration.

age of 20, creative and wilful ... and like her cousin Alice concentrated her interests and activities on her art collection and her gardens'.

Though she had homes in Monte Carlo, Paris, Ferrières, and Château de Reux in Normandy, the Villa Île de France and its fabled gardens were Béatrice's crowning achievement. Close to the villa on the west side is the Spanish Garden, with ochre walls, an arcaded loggia and flower schemes that major in the orange and yellow end of the

Preceding pages: *The garden front of Villa Île de France, seen from a circular temple at the top of the stepped water garden.*

Above: *The fountains, in a formal terraced setting beside the villa, dance in remarkable sequences in time to lively music such as Strauss waltzes.*

Right: *Venetian influences can be seen in the architecture of the ice-cream-pink villa, complemented in summer by multi-coloured impatiens, or busy lizzies.*

Above: *Water cascades down below a shaded temple set among fine pines and cedars.*

Right: *A view through the shady and colour-themed Spanish Garden.*

spectrum. Papyrus furnishes the pool among the tropical foliage of *Monstera deliciosa* and bird-like strelitzias; orange trees and dangling trumpets of datura help to suggest the ambience of a courtyard oasis in Andalucía.

Heading south from the Spanish Garden down the Florentine Alley, lined with vertical cypress trees, you reach the Jardin Lapidaire. This unusual garden is an artistically arranged architectural salvage yard of carved stone portals, Gothic windows and assorted antique masonry ranged under a huge camphor tree. It leads into a highly wrought Japanese garden, complete with carefully raked gravel, bamboo fences and a grove of cycads. The rose garden is a hillside cascade of pink blooms surmounted by a little temple, and the Exotic Garden nearby holds a collection of dramatic succulents and cacti. From the wilder, 'English' garden at the southern end, there are olive-framed views down to the bay at Saint-Jean-Cap-Ferrat.

The conception and creation of the villa was by no means straightforward. Béatrice had inherited the perfectionist Rothschild gene in spades, and though she engaged a succession of architects (eleven in all), none of their designs passed muster. She admired the Peto style with its carefully balanced references to Roman, Italian and Moorish architecture, and in the end engaged Peto's sometime colleague in Riviera work, Aaron Messiah, to design her '*palazzino*'. It took seven years, but the villa was finally completed in 1912 after much trial and error. 'She has houses built and razed in the South of France, she orders groves to be displaced and commands flowers to grow during the Mistral,' was the verdict of Elisabeth de Clermont-Tonnerre in 1928. Combining the palatial styles of Venice and Ravenna, it was largely designed by Béatrice herself, and its strawberry-ice-cream-coloured stucco seemed the inevitable choice, it being the favourite colour of someone who 'almost always wore pink dresses and seemed eternally ready to go to an elegant ball'.

Béatrice only infrequently stayed at the Villa Île de France at first, but after the death of her husband in 1916, she ceased to reside at all on Cap Ferrat, preferring Monte Carlo. She bequeathed the Villa Île de France and her art collections to the Académie des Beaux Arts, with the proviso that it be turned into a museum.

Above: *Pink, Béatrice de Rothschild's favourite colour, is much in evidence throughout the gardens and particularly among the roses.*

Right: *A white marble statue gleams against the rugged rockface.*

LA LÉOPOLDA,
NR VILLEFRANCHE

From the link road that descends in hairpin loops from the hills above the Moyenne Corniche near Villefranche, you can see that La Léopolda's 20-acre estate is something special: a sylvan haven removed from all the Riviera crowds, its clouds of silvery olive trees pierced by soaring dark fingers of impeccably pruned cypresses. Local geology helped to mark it out as a place set apart, for a steep hill on one side and a plunging ravine on the other have kept its identity separate from the busyness of Villefranche and Beaulieu.

The name derives from its purchase, more than a century ago, by King Léopold II of Belgium, a property-speculating monarch who had a passion for the Riviera and a nose for the finest sites (which led to his buying huge tracts of what was then a rather wild and undeveloped Cap Ferrat). He also had a seemingly bottomless purse with which to acquire them, funded by his perversely ruthless exploitation of the African Congo, which he regarded as being his own personal sovereign state. He created the estate of La Léopolda by acquiring, in the early

Above: *The vista along the upper garden, showing the south-facing elevations of the early-1920s house and the library. The main gardens drop down a slope to the left.*

Right: *The Peto-esque water garden, with curved colonnade and central arched loggia. Note the fine detailing of the mosaic floor and the stylish two-toned marble path leading between the ponds. The standard trees in timber tubs were clipped laurels.*

1900s, the stakeholdings of fifteen contiguous parcels of stony land dotted with old olive trees and a couple of small peasant houses. But although the property is named after him, it seems that Léopold never actually resided at La Léopolda, and he hardly ever stayed at his other great Riviera estate, Les Cèdres, close by on Cap Ferrat, preferring to sleep aboard his lavishly appointed yacht moored in the bay.

Whether he visited frequently or not, time was running out for Léopold, and after his death in 1909, his numerous properties passed to his heir, King Albert I. But the First World War was on the horizon. By 1915, huge quantities of casualties were being brought to the Riviera and, like many villas and hotels, the grounds of both La Léopolda and Les Cèdres were turned into temporary war hospitals. Around 1920, Albert I sold La Léopolda to Thérèse Vitali, the comtesse de Beauchamp, who was still the owner when *Country Life* photographed it, *circa* 1928.

Perched on the hilltop and enjoying panoramic views, the early-twentieth-century villa was laid out apparently on the footprints of the former peasant houses, comprising a harmonious set of buildings, including a single-storey library between the main house and a guesthouse. The architectural style and masterly arrangement of spaces on this difficult site suggest the influence of Harold Peto, and it is interesting to conjecture as to whether he ever offered any advice. Peto is known to have re-landscaped Les Cèdres for the Belgian king, bringing order and avenues into its grounds and creating numerous stylish garden structures, including pools and a water cascade. He was also consulted by the comtesse de Beauchamp on various projects, though she claimed La Léopolda had been all her own design.

Whatever their provenance, the disparate parts of La Léopolda's simple villa were held together by an inspired design that included a water garden of twin pools embraced by a curving colonnade (a feature that Peto used time and again, including at the Villa Maryland and Isola Bella and in England at Bridge House, Weybridge), while the library building bears a faint resemblance to a small chapel Peto created at the nearby Villa Salles.

The twin water basins were edged with seasonal flowers – blue violas in springtime – while a two-toned marble path swept directly across the neat lawns. Marking the point where the gardens dropped away from the house, a straight row of stone pillars garlanded with climbing roses led to a grand flight of grass steps, edged with stone risers, extending south-east down the hillside past several terraces containing further cultivated areas. Like other great Riviera gardens of the period, such as Villa Cypris, La Garoupe and Peto's creation at Villa Maryland, the size

of the garden and its situation on a great hillside enabled the landscaping to incorporate a dramatic stairway. The example at La Léopolda culminated in a circular pool containing an elegant single-jet fountain and a viewpoint looking across the pretty bay of Saint-Jean to the bony fingertip of the Pointe de Saint-Hospice.

Either side of this great stairway the planting was intense, comprising blue-flowered echiums, felicias, and white broom and spiraea, with pink and crimson ivy-leaved geraniums cascading over old oil jars. But what of the various terraces reached from these steps? In common with 1920s planting fashions, they were carefully colour-themed, the top layer devoted to blue and mauve tones, with a 15-foot-deep border on either side of a wide lawn, backed by sheltering olives and cypresses. Violas, primulas, nemesias, schizanthus, cinerarias and echiums filled out the borders in ascending heights; the second terrace, of yellow and orange, was planted with marigolds, eschscholzias and jasmine; the third, planted with unnamed red flowers, might well have included the popular stalwarts of venidiums, pelargoniums and crimson cinerarias.

'Spanish Gardens' were popular conceits in the Riviera at this time, and La Léopolda's was judged one of the most successful examples in its execution (its contemporaries, at Villa Île de France, *page 82*, and at Champfleuri, Cannes, still survive). It was located near the house, east of the blue terrace, through a narrow entrance in a hedge of *Cupressus macrocarpa*. Here, a long canal, edged with black and white marble tiles, was set into a smooth lawn, leading to a terracotta-red Moorish pavilion built on elegant marble pillars. Young pencil-thin cypress trees were planted in rows either side of the canal, with long strips of bedded-out *Primula malacoides* providing a frothy infill in the narrow beds at the water's edge.

Yet there was still far more to see: west of the yellow terrace, wandering paths bordered with foams of spiraea and oxalis led to the old olive groves, where the venerable trees were underplanted with sheets of bearded irises in white, blue and violet. When Euan Cox visited La Léopolda, he sagely remarked, 'We are considered lucky in our timber trees in the British Isles, but we do lack the kindly olive with its picturesque old age and its ability to grow in a soil that most of our

Above: *One of the hidden-away smaller gardens below the house, featuring a sunken lawn surrounded by a low hedge of rosemary.*

Right: *Looking between the white marble pillars of the Moorish pavilion in the Spanish Garden; themed gardens were popular in the early twentieth century. The long canal is bordered by black-and-white marble tiles and frothy clouds of* Primula malacoides.

trees would not look at. Irises seem to have a particular affinity for olives, and in some gardens this association is especially effective.' Finally, dropping a little down the hill, east of the yellow terrace was a very simple garden, 'a little sunk lawn surrounded by a thick hedge of rosemary. Stepping stones cross it, and in the middle is one enormous oil jar.'

What has become of La Léopolda since those halcyon horticultural days? These rare photographs, taken for *Country Life circa* 1928 and published in January 1929, show a Léopolda that was about to vanish. At the end of 1928 the comtesse de Beauchamp put the property up for sale, and on 1 December, *Country Life* published a full-page advertisement: 'La Leopolda ... for sale privately, or would be let for the season.' From it we learn more about the lifestyle of the owner and the finer points of its accommodation: 'The main villa comprises: large entrance hall, salon, dining room with marble table and walls panelled in marble.

Spacious sun terrace, six principal bedrooms and bathrooms en suite. Six servants' bedrooms and bathroom.' We also learn that there was a mature kitchen garden, a swimming pool and first-class hard tennis court. The secondary villa, arrived at via the semicircular cloister, had three more principal bedrooms with en suite bathrooms, and three servants' rooms. 'Every possible modern luxury is installed and there is ample garage accommodation, with chauffeur's quarters, gardener's cottage, etc.,' the agents advised.

During 1929, the villa was sold to Ogden Codman, a wealthy Bostonian architect and interior designer who had spent his childhood in France, and who had co-written *The Decoration of Houses* (1897) with Edith Wharton. Codman demolished the Léopolda of these photographs, replacing it with an elegant villa in the formal eighteenth-century style that was his trademark and completely remodelling the formerly labour-intensive grounds. Unlike many of the Riviera estates of the belle époque, La Léopolda has managed to hold on to its substantial acreage, and it remains one of the most glamorous and sought-after properties in the Mediterranean, concealed from prying eyes by high walls and a filigree veil of old olive trees springing out of immaculate emerald lawns.

Left: *A rustic path leads through the wilder gardens between tall cypress trees, cleared of their lower branches so they appear to be on stilts.*

Below: *A circular fountain pool fringed with pink Bellis daisies was reached at the bottom of a great stairway leading down from lawns near the house. The views stretch across the bay of Saint-Jean-Cap-Ferrat to the bony finger of Pointe St-Hospice.*

VILLA CYPRIS, CAP MARTIN

Exclusive Cap Martin, a promontory of sun-bleached limestone forested with characterful pines, was until 1861 (when the Roquebrune area came under French rule) the hunting ground of the princes of Monaco, who had hunted stags there. But in the latter third of the nineteenth century, pigeon-shooting had become such a big draw for the Riviera's *hivernants* that in 1886 the wilds of Cap Martin were obtained for a shooting enterprise, whereby visitors who regretted leaving behind the Scottish moors each winter could at least take a potshot at the copious rabbits and pheasants. But the 'land of the big green turtle' – as the Empress Eugénie, widow of Napoleon III, aptly described it – became so valuable for Riviera development that in 1889 it was acquired by an English real-estate syndicate. Thus commenced the portioning-out of land and the building of a series of great villas set in ample gardens.

Among them were the Andalucían-born Empress's own Villa Cyrnos and, next door, the Villa Cypris, built for Mme Cyprienne Hériot Douine by the French architect Edouard Arnaud. Set in 10 acres of open pine forest on the south-western side of the Cap, the pale-grey stone and marble villa was built at the top of a hill, with its gardens dropping steadily down to the water's edge, taking in grand views of Monaco and Monte Carlo across the broad bay.

Dramatic stairways feature in a good number of Mediterranean gardens – more often than not, the terrain is best managed this way. But there cannot be many rivals able to compete for sheer spectacle with the Villa Cypris's three parallel flights of stairs. One was aligned dead-centre with the symmetrical villa, linking it to the sea far below; the

Above: *The magnificent galleried cloister set above the thrashing waters of the bay. The cloister has a chapel at each end. It can only be reached via the bridge shown in the foreground.*

Left: *The smaller, L-shaped loggia on the edge of the wild garden, with westerly views across the water to Monaco. Note Mainella's careful detailing in the stonework and brickwork.*

other two led away from either side of the villa and were intersected halfway down by snaking garden paths leading to differently themed areas of the grounds. Each step of each stairway was turfed – tricky and labour-intensive to mow – and edged with stone risers; a ribbon of seasonal flowers was planted down the centre of each stairway to form a colourful band streaking through the grassy steps. The central flight was particularly fine, bordered with carved marble columns crowned by stern marble eagles and falcons. Marigolds rippled in a golden strip down the centre, terminating at a mosaic-floored landing with a central marble font, while on either side the steps were bordered all the way down with pink roses, night-scented stocks and clusters of freesias; as well as being visually arresting, this was clearly a garden where sweet floral fragrances mingled in the twilight air with the spicier scents of the *maquis*.

For the gardens (and also the villa interiors), Mme Douine engaged the Campania-born Venetian painter Raffaële Mainella, a gifted if eclectic designer whom Ferdinand Bac later pithily dismissed as an 'architect from Naples and former hairdresser's assistant ...'. Mainella brought his ambitious designs to Villa Cypris and also to a nearby property, Torre Clementina, favouring a heady cocktail of the Roman, Byzantine, Arabic and medieval styles he had grown up among in the vicinity of Naples. Describing Torre Clementina, which had been built for the heiress and socialite Ernesta Stern, Bac noted Mainella had plundered the decorative influences of 'China and Japan, Syracuse and Trebizond, not to mention the translucent marbles of San Miniato ... there is an accumulation of effects lacking nothing but a degree of Christian restraint ...'.

Actually, the same could be said of Villa Cypris, but Christian restraint was not what Mainella's clients expected from him; for that they could have gone to Harold Peto or Achille Duchêne. At Villa Cypris, Mainella made sense of the site by putting in the aforementioned stairways, the central one leading to his *pièce de résistance*: a massive brick bridge and colonnaded cloister gallery built high above the sea, where cross currents cause foamy surf to crash on to the rocks. It is hard to imagine a more alluring invitation to descend that floral flight of steps. At each end of the colonnade he built a small chapel entered by handsome wrought-copper doors between twisted marble pillars, with a little bell tower at its centre.

'The garden houses are extremely beautiful features of this place,' wrote Margherita Ballance in *Country Life*'s article of 1927. 'The colonnade consists of twenty-two small Romanesque arches on each side, all the columns being of varied material and design, many being of porphyry. The colonnade actually hangs over the sea, with its myriad changes of aspect and colouring; and, at the same time, the graceful Riviera pine and bright-leaved pittosporum, with its waxen flowers, lend a becoming frame to the landward side. The cloister is roofed with the rounded local tiles, the interior being of dark stained beams. ... The only means of approach to the sea-cloister is by the brick and stone

The great central stairway (one of three parallel sets of steps) in its heyday, aligned on the centre of the villa. Each stair was turfed with grass. Seasonal flowers decorate the sides and magnificent sculpted raptors increase the sense of grandeur.

bridge, with its little carved stone lions and touches of Provençal tile work.'

A path leading eastwards from the bridge up the steep hillside snaked towards another handsomely colonnaded building: the L-shaped lookout known as the Venetian Temple, set among old pines and yellow broom. Heading north from there up a woodland path, you would arrive at a formal Dutch-style water garden and, beside it under the trees, a romantic 'ruin' described as a pergola, though it was much grander than that, being modelled on the Moorish interior of the Great Mosque at Córdoba, with striped marble and brick arches bearing down on sixteen carved marble stilts, the whole festooned with climbing roses and jasmine, and underplanted with forget-me-nots.

These adaptations of design templates from other lands were not

Above: A relaxed and shady woodland walk through the wild garden.

Left above: The approach to the L-shaped loggia, with the sea off to the right and the woodland garden of old pines and olives on the left and behind the structure.

Left below: The Moorish pergola, a remarkable folly with horseshoe arches based on those in the Great Mosque of Córdoba. They bear down on sixteen carved marble stilts.

unusual in the Riviera at that period, though Villa Cypris's examples are particularly lavish. Mme Vagliano had her Spanish, Moorish, Dutch and Japanese gardens in her spacious grounds at Cannes; Béatrice de Rothschild imported a similarly diverse range of gardens into her 18-acre hilltop on Cap Ferrat (*see page 82*). Even Lawrence Johnston could not resist tucking away a Moorish garden near the woods at Serre de la Madone (*see page 114*) or laying out a formal Dutch-style parterre filled with *clusiana* tulips.

Margherita Ballance's description of the Dutch-style sunk garden and its environs in the north-eastern corner of the Villa Cypris grounds reveals the extent to which even a small part of these gardens demanded skilled and painstaking work to show off the property at its best in late winter and spring: 'Through the centre a wide band of water in a blue-tinted canal respects the trees towering above. The square beds are box-edged, with clipped sugar-loaves of yew at each corner. The vivid shades of orange nemesia set around a mist of forget-me-nots is the scheme of some of these parterres, and others have the favourite red daisy as the centre, with a band of green grass as contrast. The whole of the sunk garden is paved with brick; here and there, where the box runs to a point, tall iron stands with pots of schizanthus fill the blanks. At intervals along the edge of the canal square boxes are let in on a level with the pavement, containing large plants of *Senecio multibracteata*, with its fine foliage and golden flowers.' The sunk garden was accessed by little stairways of white marble and brick; one end featured a fountain inspired by Chinese-lantern design, and the whole area was 'rich in unusual garden ornaments: colour and contrast being the decisive factors in the arrangement. These are good guides in a climate and environment where both are so lavishly at the disposal of the architect and the gardener.'

What Mrs Ballance did not refer to, however, was the singular character of the villa's owner, who was quite as intriguing as her garden. Mme Douine – widely recognised as Émile Zola's model for his rags-to-riches story *Au Bonheur des Dames* – had been a young salesgirl at the Grands Magasins du Louvre who captured the heart of and married the wealthy owner, Olympe Hériot, an astute businessman a generation older than herself. By 1885, she had inherited the three-storey Parisian department store, among other enterprises, and an ever-burgeoning bank balance. She was later remarried to Robert Douine. Her daughter, Virginie Hériot, became a legend in the sailing world in the 1920s; the lookout points at Villa Cypris – the open lawns immediately below the house and the coastal colonnaded buildings – provided ample opportunity for Mme Douine to watch her daughter tacking back and forth out at sea.

It is fascinating to see how Villa Cypris looks today, almost exactly a century on from its original creation. Like nearly all of its contemporaries, it suffered in the last half of the twentieth century from a dramatically reduced maintenance staff. Most of its transportable artefacts have disappeared. But the core of the garden – its stairways, colonnaded buildings, deliciously snaking woodland paths, its formal garden and Moorish 'pergola' – has survived relatively intact. Today, huge investment has been poured into regenerating and partially redesigning the garden (a rocky 'mountain stream' and a rhododendron glade thriving on imported acidic soil are among its new features). Investment is needed to restore the wonderful brick and porphyry colonnades, which have suffered substantial weather erosion in this coastal location.

Villa Cypris remains a treasured and unique property in a location of rare beauty almost unparalleled on the northern shores of the Mediterranean. Historical records of the gardens reveal the careful juxtaposition of its preserved areas of wilderness – the natural flora of the locality, its pines and Mediterranean scrub – beside Mainella's more exotic creations. If its areas of natural landscape are thoughtfully preserved alongside the intensively gardened ones, then its future as one of the great Riviera gardens will be assured.

The formal 'Dutch' garden, with long canal and topiaries. Note the Moorish pergola hidden away in the far corner on the left, backed by the magnificent natural forest of Cap Martin. Much later, this garden was altered and the canal widened to form a swimming pool.

VILLA NOAILLES, HYÈRES

Several of the Riviera gardens in this book were made in the 1920s – Lawrence Johnston's Serre de la Madone and Consuelo Vanderbilt Balsan's Lou Sueil, for example, as well as Edith Wharton's Sainte-Claire le Château – but none of them speak of the Jazz Age like the garden of Villa Noailles. Edith Wharton's romantic garden with its subtle suggestions of a Tuscan fortress was just a short stroll away, the other side of the feudal castle ruins that dominate the hill upon which both Villa Noailles and Sainte-Claire sit. But whereas Johnston, Balsan and Wharton were Edwardians – Victorians, even – with all that that implied emotionally and artistically, the vicomte de Noailles was of the next generation, having come to Hyères in his early thirties in 1923 to build his new villa and garden.

Charles de Noailles and his wife, Marie-Laure, were part of the post-war experimental art world, and their arrival in Hyères brought a breath of fresh air. They counted Surrealist painters, sculptors, jazz musicians, avant-garde film-makers and Modernist designers among their vibrant circle of friends. Though Charles de Noailles was already a keen and knowledgeable gardener (it is said that he cultivated annual flowers in the trenches during the First World War), it was his interest in Modernism that led him to commission a radical new villa in his Parc St-Bernard from the architect Robert Mallet-Stevens – the first commission for the youngish architect, who was an exact contemporary of Le Corbusier.

By 1925, the boxy villa, with its interlocking planes and volumes and square-framed green courtyard, was ready and Charles de Noailles began to plan the gardens. Inspired by the triangular garden he saw at the Exposition Internationale des Arts Décoratifs in Paris, *The Garden of Water and Light* designed by the Armenian architect Gabriel Guévrékian, he immediately commissioned a copy. It was undiluted Art Deco and perfectly suited to de Noailles' Modernist villa, while its triangular shape was ideal for squeezing into the space available at the lower level, in front of the Green Drawing Room.

This strange garden has become an icon of its age: unique, instantly recognisable, and a source of inspiration for one or two other Art Deco gardens – notably, High and Over in Buckinghamshire – as well as for some of the more experimental gardens displayed in recent years at the annual Festival des Jardins at Chaumont-sur-Loire. Like the most intricately worked knot garden of Tudor times, this confection seemed made for viewing from above – a fact not lost on Charles de Noailles, who had it situated where it could be peered over like the prow of a ship from the 'deck' of the lawned courtyard a storey above. But to reach it and wander up through its cleverly stepped arrangement you needed to go downstairs and out through the drawing room.

Flat planes of colour were introduced with ceramic tiles of red, yellow, grey and blue, and a path of violet mosaic. Triangular-shaped plant containers organised in a zigzag pattern were filled with foliage plants of two contrasting shades of green. Yet the use of plants in this garden was sparing (fortunately for Charles de Noailles, there were several other garden areas around the villa in which he could indulge his passion for plants in great variety). One of its features, adding further movement to the optical illusions created by Guévrékian, was an obliquely erotic kinetic sculpture, known as *Joy of Living*, by the Lithuanian-born Cubist sculptor Jacques Lipchitz.

In contrast to the lack of plant life in the Cubist garden and the apparent sterility of the villa with its unadorned elevations, flowers were especially appreciated and carefully arranged in the house. Even so, the interior decoration was of minimalist severity, so as not to compromise the purity of the architecture, to the extent that works of art by the de Noailles' friends – Miró, Picasso, Chagall, Braque and others – were put on display only on rare occasions.

Above: *The walled and lawned courtyard immediately outside the villa. It was a daringly minimalist composition for the times, with 'window' openings overlooking the garden created by Gabriel Guévrékian in 1925.*

Left: *The steep site is managed with strong retaining walls and lightly shaded here and there by the ubiquitous pine trees of the region.*

Charles de Noailles was passionate about plants, displaying 'an insatiable appetite for gardens' throughout his long life and even being awarded the honour of a vice-presidency of the Royal Horticultural Society, as well as becoming president of the International Dendrological Society. As Vivian Russell pointed out, 'He had begun by planting unsuitable and brightly coloured bulbs under cork oaks in the *maquis* high up at Hyères, and ended up the master plantsman, his garden a distillation of all that he had absorbed in his long aesthetic life – what he liked, what suited, what wanted to grow. He brought both novelty and wisdom, and he thought of the garden in all of its dimensions: the sound and smell of a garden as well as the look of it.'

Beyond the rigours of the Cubist garden, the grounds were more richly and romantically planted. Almond trees and olives which had 'been there forever' brought structural qualities to the borders of the terraces, and that ubiquitous rose of the Riviera, 'General Schablikine', trailed its flamboyant pink blossoms through the springtime. Abundant sun-loving flowers created a long season of colour, with venidiums, cistus, abutilons, salvias and tough succulents basking in the heat.

The broiling sun and the salt-laden air, however, proved too much for Charles de Noailles in the end, and after the Second World War he retreated to his other home in the hills of Grasse to cultivate a more temperate range of plants, including magnolias, camellias, halesia, davidia and dogwood.

The Villa Noailles and surrounding Parc St-Bernard are today owned and maintained by the town of Hyères and open to visitors, who can still admire Guévrékian's strange creation and the Noailles' interesting collections of Mediterranean plants which thrive on the surrounding slopes.

Above: *With its flat planes and boxy construction, the Villa Noailles was, stylistically, the antithesis of Edith Wharton's ancient château across the hill.*

Left: *Gabriel Guévrékian's innovative* Garden of Water and Light, *with its abstract geometry, was exhibited at the 1925 Paris Exposition Internationale des Arts Décoratifs and then re-created at the Villa Noailles. More restoration has taken place since these photographs were taken.*

VILLA SYLVIA, CAP FERRAT

There is much that is remarkable about the Villa Sylvia, built by Harold Peto in 1902. For a start, there is its dramatic position. It was shoe-horned into a narrow and steeply sloping site between the main road running through the bottlenecked north end of Cap Ferrat and the fabulous Baie de l'Espalmadour, looking westwards across to Villefranche.

Unconcerned by any potential intrusion from traffic in this newly popular peninsula, Peto positioned the villa at the top of the site, jammed right next to the road; but in doing so, he enabled the gardens – which he also designed – to appear generous and dramatic, as they descended in terraces and olive-wooded slopes down to the sea. As H. Avray Tipping pointed out in his article of 1910 (the first of *Country Life*'s articles on Riviera properties): 'Had some sort of winding drive from the high embanked road been contrived as an approach to the house, much of the precious ground would have been taken up in an uninteresting manner, and the house would not have commanded all its garden and used it as a foreground to the blue sea below and the hillsides opposite.'

Peto's client for this project was the wealthy American painter Ralph Wormeley Curtis (1854–1922), a cousin of John Singer Sargent and a friend of Henry James, Edith Wharton and the art collector Isabella Stewart Gardner. The brief to the architect had been to create a house and garden that could be comfortably lived in (albeit by the exacting standards of the Edwardian *beau monde*), and Curtis could not have chosen anyone better to realise his dreams of a fine winter home in this superb location.

Peto's villa (which was named after the Curtises' daughter, Sylvia) drew its inspiration directly from the Italian palaces with which he (and his client) were so familiar, creating an imposing interior stairway leading from the entrance hall and upper rooms down to the *salons* and extensive gardens beyond. And in giving the house a long alignment on the north–south axis, he enabled all of the key rooms of the villa to enjoy open, westerly views, especially from a central, vaulted loggia and the balustraded terrace above it.

Tipping described the loggia as 'a triple arcade built of a finely varied, open-grained ashlar stone. It is the same as that which the Romans used for the great Pont du Gard Aqueduct, and resembles the product of our own Ham Hill quarries.' This last reference would have pleased Peto as much as anything, for he frequently used the warm-coloured limestone of Somerset's Ham Hill in his English projects. From the west loggia, flights of steps descended to the terrace, where all the walls and balustradings in the vicinity were smothered in April by the large white blooms of *Rosa laevigata*, a Chinese species found all over the

Villa Sylvia viewed from its south-western corner in 1910. Built in 1902, its garden already shows a great deal of maturity. Rhododendrons were grown in special ericaceous compost in wooden tubs. Note the characterful olive tree and elegant garden bench.

Riviera, and its pink-flowered hybrid 'Anemonenrose' (also known as 'Pink Cherokee'), which had been bred in the 1890s.

Head southwards, round the corner of the villa, and you would find the only truly formal part of the gardens: a little four-square arrangement of beds set into pressed gravel paths between a long run of the rose pergola to the west and the high wall retaining the road to the east. *Country Life*'s 1910 photographs reveal the beds packed out with fragrant pansies and violas in full bloom, with clipped conifers marking the corners and a central small bed devoted to a lemon tree (though later photographs from the 1920s showed this had been replaced by a large oil-jar centrepiece).

All of the remaining ground between villa and sea was treated informally. Most of the fine and characterful old olive trees were

Above: The south garden in 1910, with formal beds filled with fragrant pansies and violas. The house was built right next to the road, its upper storey level with the street, enabling the gardens to flow uninterrupted down to the seashore on the left-hand side.

Left: Inside the western loggia, built of open-grained ashlar stone. The outer balustrade is engulfed in various spring-flowering roses, such as R. laevigata *and* 'Anemonenrose'.

retained, and grassy paths were woven among them, leading the visitor past great swathes of spring bulbs – crocuses, narcissus and anemones, whose pageant was followed by a grand finale of irises flowering prodigiously in April, just as the owners would be preparing to pack up and move on to pastures new for the summer season.

Tipping pointed out that no less striking than the old olives were the pine trees, 'which at one end of the ground overhang the water in a manner which would arouse the admiration of a Japanese gardener'. Revealing the impeccable taste of the architect and the owners in not over-gardening this wonderful site, Tipping noted that 'All this tract has been left half wild', though spring-flowering shrubs, including magnolias and tree peonies, had been planted as highlights here and there. 'Orange and lemon trees bear their bright-coloured burden, and great clumps of New Zealand Flax give form and rigidity to the general picture of graceful growths ...' wrote Tipping. 'But there is no attempt to make the garden merely exotic, and many a tree and plant that does well in our climate is here introduced, and only differs in its earlier, and sometimes more profuse, blooming.'

When *Country Life* revisited Villa Sylvia in the late 1920s, the gardens were, if anything, even more beautiful, having matured and been carefully maintained by Ralph Curtis's widow, Lisa (née Colt, an heiress of the Colt firearms dynasty). It was noted that Peto's original garden designs and colour schemes had been so good that they were still used twenty-five years later, though of course the planting had moved on, for Mrs Curtis was also an accomplished gardener.

The interiors, too, were much as they had been when Peto designed and furnished them, and Whistler's famously luminous 1898 portrait of the young Mrs Ralph Curtis (now in the Cleveland Museum of Art, Ohio) still dominated the south end of the *salon*. This portrait, Sargent's wedding gift to the Curtises, lit up the *salon* as effectively as the huge arcaded windows in the west wall.

An interesting point about Villa Sylvia, as described by Tipping in 1910, is that he used the house and its garden as an opportunity to encourage better-quality design in a region that had seen prodigious amounts of ill-conceived construction for more than fifty years. 'It strikes us, when we first hopefully inspect the numberless houses and gardens that throng round Cannes and Mentone and dot the whole coast-line between these two towns, that, however enjoyable they may be, they might certainly have been better,' he warned. 'The conclusion is forced upon us that the problem of how the house and garden should be created so that it may exactly assimilate to the environment that Nature and history have given has, in most cases, not been solved. Neither the loud and showy villa of the Northern French watering-place nor the ordinary run of Victorian English country house strikes the right note hereabouts.'

Villa Sylvia remains one of the most glorious properties of Cap Ferrat. The blue-green pantiled roof announces its presence even from across the bay at Villefranche, and although it now has a different name, the villa and the vestiges of its garden are, more than a century on, testament to the genius of Harold Peto in the Mediterranean.

Right: Arum lilies and dramatic strelitzias ornament a pool at the north end of the villa. Note Peto's eye for perfect detail in the series of elegant jars atop the balustrade.

Below: The view south towards the steps into the lower gardens. Harold Peto retained the olive and pine trees and created informal paths winding through them among swathes of spring bulbs and irises. As the new century progressed, such 'wild' plantings gained popularity.

SERRE DE LA MADONE, MENTON

The intriguing name of this property needs some clarification. It is often called La Serre de la Madone, meaning the greenhouse of the Madonna, which does not seem implausible in the context of its beautiful garden. From the mid-1920s to the mid-1950s, its owner and creator, Lawrence Johnston, raised all his treasured tender plants here in the sheltered climate of Menton.

The name is more prosaic than that, however: in fact it refers to *Le Serre de la Madone*, a narrow ridge of pointy mountains. Since Major Johnston's small estate on a steep hillside of the Gorbio valley occupies the site of an old hamlet called Le Serre de la Madone, after the mountain that sheltered it, he simply adopted the ancient title. Nevertheless, in the documents preserved by Mme Bottin, the daughter of Johnston's head gardener, the owner always referred to his domain simply as Serre de la Madone, without a definite article attached, no

Above: The ochre-coloured farmhouse, extended by Lawrence Johnston into a substantial villa. Its gardens have recently undergone a magnificent programme of restoration.

Left: The Plane Tree Garden, a simple, four-square parterre. In Lawrence Johnston's time, the four sections were filled in with carpets of double-flowered periwinkles and red-and-white tulips.

doubt enjoying the ambiguity of the name in the context of his exotic plant collection.

Perched on a south-west-facing slope behind Menton, the garden was all but destroyed after Johnston's death in 1958, when its vast plant collection was uprooted and redistributed. In recent years, though, a compelling and important restoration has been undertaken after the garden – dismantled, overgrown, and, in the 1990s, in danger of being built over – was bought in 1999 by the Conservatoire du Littoral, aided by contributions from the town of Menton and several other benefactors. Such is the garden's importance, it was designated a Historic Monument in France.

It is a fascinating restoration because Johnston had also created the world-famous Hidcote Manor gardens in Gloucestershire; those at Serre de la Madone reveal a different facet of one of horticulture's most enigmatic figures. And it is important, too, because for more than three decades the garden here was a repository of his rarest plant collections. All the delicate species that would not survive on the cold, remote hilltop farmstead of Hidcote Bartrim, where Johnston had been making a garden since 1907, could be gathered and grown among the lemons and olives in the nurturing warmth of Menton.

Here, between the wars, the slender, blue-eyed and energetic 'Johnnie' Johnston was truly among his own kind, including fellow American gardeners such as Edith Wharton at Hyères and Consuelo Vanderbilt Balsan at Èze, the vicomte de Noailles, also at Hyères, and the Warres at Roquebrune, to name but a few of his wide circle of Riviera gardening friends. They took plant-hunters' picnics into the Alpes-Maritimes and swapped plants, cuttings and seeds of wisdom. In 1935 Edith Wharton asked the Pulitzer Prize-winning novelist Louis Bromfield if he knew the Spanish rose called 'Apelles Mestres': 'Lawrence Johnston tells me it is the most beautiful rose in the world.'

The Gorbio valley hillside was in many respects an ideal place to make a garden. It had been terraced since ancient times for the cultivation of olives and grapes; rainfall was reliably high in the key growing seasons of autumn and spring; and the gradient enabled the land to be freely draining. Climate-wise, Menton was considered to be the mildest and most protected section of the Riviera, as the local physician Dr J. Henry Bennet had been at great pains to point out in his *Winter and Spring on the Shores of the Mediterranean*, much read in the 1860s and 1870s.

The house, a typical old farmhouse, sits near the top of its garden, with a sheltering forest rising up behind it. Johnston extended his home by adding large wings on either side and made it more comfortable, for the original point of being on the Riviera was to be with his invalided mother, the wealthy widow Gertrude Winthrop. Outdoors some twenty-three gardeners and stonemasons worked through the second half of the 1920s, reinforcing the retaining walls of the terraces, creating a long vista which descended from the centre of the house, and fashioning a range of differently themed garden areas. Even in the years leading up to the Second World War, there were still twelve gardeners fully employed here.

As at Hidcote, the arrangement of various garden 'rooms' enabled different moods to be conjured up and the widest possible range of plants to be catered for in a stylish setting. In one area, water would predominate; in another, it would be brilliant sunshine; elsewhere, cool shade. A fashionably Moorish garden was built near the woods behind the house, with an arched loggia erected to display Johnston's collection of colourful glazed tiles. His taste for the exotic was also indulged with an enormous aviary, the home of ibis, parrots and crowned cranes from Africa, among its more flamboyant inhabitants. Nearby, the wisteria-garlanded belvedere was a winter suntrap, taking in wonderful views of garden and house. There were rock gardens, a pergola walk, fountains, glasshouses for the tenderest plants, and a formidable quantity of different species, all growing amid the natural beauty of umbrella pines, vertical cypresses and cascading pepper trees.

Serre de la Madone's central stairway provided the key axis, leading down to rectangular pools furnished with water lilies, papyrus and lotus blossoms, and below them to one side was the Plane Tree Garden.

At the bottom of the great central stairway lie the rectangular pools, filled with water lilies, papyrus and lotus blossoms. Provençal 'Anduze' vases are lined up on either side.

This comprised a four-square simple parterre, planted with the sort of restraint we see in Hidcote's more restful areas; in Johnston's day, each quarter was filled with carpets of the double form of purple periwinkle and the springtime flourish of thousands of red-and-white *Tulipa clusiana*. A single umbrella-pruned plane tree rises out of each bed, bringing shade just in time for summer's heat.

Johnston is often described as shy and secretive, and somebody who did not write anything down. This cannot be maintained any longer, though there are scant surviving records since his heir, Nancy Lindsay, destroyed them after his death. The recent exciting discovery of three slim volumes – his notebook covering the years 1925 to 1928, and two engagement diaries for 1929 and 1932 – reveal in his own hand, and contrary to speculation, a man who led an active social life, especially lunch and tennis parties on three or four days a week.

He also kept meticulous notes about everything. For example, travelling on 16 September 1926 from Hidcote to Serre de la Madone, he jotted down expenses: £9 9s 3d for luggage to Menton; 5s 6d for porters on the boat; Ffr100 to 'Maurice for passing us through customs'; and, on more than one occasion, Ffr6 for grapes. It cost £3 in England and Ffr659 in France to bring his chauffeur Ernest to Menton; later, staff at Menton received Christmas bonuses: £2 for Ernest and also for Ellen, a maid, and Ffr400 for the Italian servants.

Mrs Winthrop died in December 1926, so there was not the usual need to rush to Menton the following autumn. Instead, Johnston organised a three-month-long plant-hunting trip to South Africa. A quarter of a century earlier, he had seen what the South African flora had to offer, having served in the Second Boer War from 1900 to 1902. This time it was a peaceful (if slightly competitive) expedition, in the company of fellow gardeners Major Collingwood 'Cherry' Ingram, Reginald Cory of Cothay Manor, and George Taylor (later Sir George Taylor, director of the Royal Botanical Gardens). Sailing out from Southampton on 2 September, a few weeks before Johnston's fifty-sixth birthday, this was to be a particularly valuable and rewarding trip for him, as so much of the Cape flora could be expected to thrive outdoors at Serre de la Madone. It was also done in some comfort and style, since Johnston had brought along his chauffeur and his valet and had organised two cars – a Jeep and a Buick, to await their arrival in the Cape.

Lawrence Johnston's notebook reveals that the party took in a visit to Kirstenbosch Botanical Gardens and a number of Cape Province towns before heading for the coast – Mossel Bay, Knysna and Port Elizabeth. Later, they explored the Drakensberg range, while Cherry Ingram

mentions in his memoirs their day's visit to Doornkloof, the farm of General Jan Smuts, near Pretoria; they were well received, since the general was an avid botanist (though Frau Smuts, understandably, 'hardly troubled to disguise the fact that she still remembered the Boer War'). Ingram was amazed at 'the extraordinary number and variety' of species in the South African flora, 'immensely rich in beautiful flowering plants'. His chief interest was in collecting unusual species of gladiolus, but their searches, 'ranging back and forth ... for all the world like a couple of questing pointers searching for grouse on a Scottish moor', produced much else, including species of aloe, cotyledon, cyrtanthus, felicia, hypoxis, ipomoea, jasminum, kniphofia, lobelia, leucospermum and cyathea, which Johnston cultivated both at Hidcote (where he had a winter plant house for tender species) and at Serre de la Madone, which was the principal repository for his South African collection.

Later quests for garden plants saw Johnston heading to Mount Kilimanjaro (in February 1929, when he noted: 'The boys nearly burnt the hut down by making too big a fire'). He also joined George Forrest in 1931 on his gruelling last expedition to Yunnan, China, where they collected *Jasminum polyanthum* and seeds of *Mahonia siamensis* (now the signature plant of Serre de la Madone) and *M. lomariifolia*.

Lawrence Johnston passed Hidcote to the National Trust and put down permanent roots at Serre de la Madone in 1948, moving his whole household, including his beloved pack of dachshunds, to Menton, where he lived until his death in 1958. Nancy Lindsay, the daughter of Johnston's great friend Norah Lindsay, inherited Serre de la Madone but decided to sell it, though she invited the Cambridge Botanic Gardens to come and take away any plants they wanted from it first. Fortunately, this meant that the Cambridge accession sheets provided a precise record of Johnston's prodigious collections of 'rare trees, shrubs and an incalculable number of herbaceous plants and bulbs which rivalled those at Hanbury', and the garden still possessed a number of the original plants. Now that Serre de la Madone's future is assured, a symbiotic relationship has been formed between Cambridge, Hidcote and Menton, and Lawrence Johnston's 'lost' garden is now very much back on the Riviera map.

Above: *The simply constructed pergola walk, recently restored.*

Right: *The sculptural beauty of the lotus flower,* Nelumbo nucifera, *now once again a spectacular feature of the water gardens at Serre de la Madone.*

On the vigil of a great winter fiesta the little town of Corfu is as lively as an ant heap; peasants and townspeople alike busy providing for the coming holidays. The narrow streets are half blocked with stacks of fruit and vegetables, and overflowing stalls of all manner of provisions. There are pyramids of endive, cauliflowers and broccoli in all its charming and original shades of mauve, yellow and purple; enormous faggots of leeks and of all the good wild green things; masses of oranges and lemons glowing from their fresh shining leaves; stalls of dried fruits and nuts.

Sophie Atkinson, *An Artist in Corfu*

Greece

The roof of Cavogallo, surrounded by protective olive trees, looking over the serene waters of the Bay of Messina.

GASTOURI, CORFU

On the Ionian island of Corfu, the olive trees grow unchecked, casting a shimmering silver-green mantle over the hills, dotted with exclamation marks of darkest-green cypress. Tucked in among them is Gastouri, owned by Cali Doxiadis, who bought the handsome eighteenth-century farmhouse with its attendant vineyard and olive groves more than three decades ago from Michael and Mirabel Osler, as a place to retreat from the hurly-burly of Athens.

Initially, it was somewhere to potter and make a garden of sorts, though the task was almost Herculean in the early years. The water supply was desperately limited, and the relentless Corfiot summer proved too broiling for the owner to achieve her early 'dream vision' of an English-style cottage garden resplendent with roses, phlox and delphiniums. The problem was compounded by the fact that it was for many years a holiday home and therefore not somewhere receiving daily nurture. There was also more urgent work to be done in the first years: re-banking the terraced landscape and refurbishing the interiors.

The breakthrough came twenty years ago, when Cali Doxiadis turned her attention to cultivating a garden of plants more naturally attuned to

Mediterranean conditions: cistus and lavenders, bulbs, thymes, oleanders, rosemaries and scented-leaf pelargoniums. Oddly enough, with that change of direction, the walled garden has now largely achieved the desired cottage-garden feel (although one flavoured by the local climate), with an eclectic and thriving mix of flowers, culinary herbs, a few salads and fruiting trees. Those trees produce lemons, walnuts, avocado pears and figs, and among them are sun-basking eschscholzias, zinnias, salvias, verbenas and perilla.

The Tuscan-style farmhouse, with its ochre-rendered walls and handsome double stairway engulfed by star jasmine, sits well back from the road on levelled ground beyond citrus orchards. Thick walls enclose its west-facing flower garden, with less intensively planted areas beyond. Around the entrance door there are pots of assorted succulents and fragrant gardenia, plump hydrangeas and purple tradescantia. The best

Above: *The sunny garden in front of the farmhouse hosts a changing tableau of annuals from year to year; in this instance, calendulas and zinnias create a fiery vision.*

Right: *Laden with lemons: the abundant citrus fruits are located conveniently near the farmhouse kitchen.*

use was made of the materials to hand: stones dug out of the fields were used for walling and making raised beds; and smooth, curved millstones from the old wine and olive presses were transformed into garden seats and tables, placed in conversational arrangements.

The walled garden is also a hive of production, since Cali, aided by local horticulturist Roy Sanders, grows everything from seeds and cuttings nurtured in a cold-frame. This splendidly robust, low construction of hardwood and glass, referred to as 'Lenin's tomb', is always sheltering seedlings: they include special plants, such as *Echium wildpretii*, a flamboyant native of Tenerife, the rare bigeneric hybrid *Amarcrinum Howardii*, which produces clutches of exquisite pale-pink trumpets at the top of each stout stem, and numerous aromatic basils destined for the kitchen.

Through a gateway in the south wall are gravel-mulched beds beside a swimming pool, one of which is home to an intriguing scree garden of prostrate rosemaries. They were originally planted on their sides, so that

Left: *Living sculpture – a magnificent olive tree, one of the many characterful examples that enhance the small estate. Birds and small mammals find sanctuary in the crevices.*

Below: *Assorted hydrangeas are grown in pots so that they can be given a richer soil and moved into the shade when necessary, cooled by draughts of air brought through the house.*

the branches swerve upwards before tumbling like dreadlocks to the ground. The effect is of a sociable gathering of aromatic Mediterranean 'bonsais' among characterful boulders and squat junipers. Another gravelled bed hosts a glorious wave of deep-red hemerocallis planted among helichrysums and lavenders. The main lavender collection, however, is bedded into a graded bank facing the distant sea, with *Lavandula angustifolia*, *dentata* and *stoechas* types in great variety.

Away from the immediate environs of the house and its walled garden, where colourful and exotic flowers predominate, Cali Doxiadis – who is currently the president of the Mediterranean Garden Society – has blended the gardens seamlessly into the broader landscape of olive groves, with a selection of native and typical *maquis* plants. Extensive work in refurbishing an old olive-press barn on the edge of the property has produced further planting opportunities. A rugged rock bank (spoil from the necessary excavations) is clothed with cistuses, thymes, euphorbias and santolinas, with added agaves and gazanias; it is approached through a grove of oleanders, lentisc, brooms and cypress trees. Beds around the ancient olive trees nearby erupt with locally naturalised tazetta narcissi in winter, followed by germanica-type wild irises in spring and, in autumn, native *Cyclamen hederifolium*.

CAVOGALLO, PELOPONNESE

In building Cavogallo and its elegant garden, the architect and garden designer Charles Shoup created something that had not hitherto existed: a plausible style for a 'traditional' Greek country house. Unlike England, and, indeed, other parts of Europe, Greece does not have a tradition of grand country houses: the country is the domain of hard-working farms, of olive groves and vineyards, while smart houses belong in cities – and more precisely, in Athens.

Yet here is wonderful Cavogallo, majestically spread out on a hillside overlooking the Bay of Messinia. Mr Shoup completed it in 1992, though he started planting the site long before, in 1971. Taking the long view, he had in mind to remove himself from Athens, where he had lived for many years, to the wildly beautiful, flower-rich limestone landscapes and olive groves of the Mani, the southernmost peninsula of the Peloponnese.

The writer Patrick Leigh Fermor, a long-time resident of this part of the Mani, revealed its singular appeal back in 1958: 'Cooled in summer by the breeze from the gulf, the great screen of the Taygetus shuts out

intruding winds from the north and the east; no tramontana can reach it. It is like those Elysian confines of the world where Homer says that life is easiest for men; where no snow falls, no strong winds blow nor rain comes down, but the melodious west wind blows for ever from the sea to bring coolness to those who live there. ... No wonder the nereids made it their home.' But the Mani's topography – hemmed in by the sea and cut off from more accessible Greece by the towering Taygetus mountains – ensures that it has remained a popular destination for discerning visitors.

Cavogallo's 37 steep and stony acres reach down to the water's edge, with figs, pomegranates, lemons, plums and palms adding to the silvery canopies of the olives. Mr Shoup has also carefully introduced vertical cypresses into the scheme, as they have such an affinity with Classical architecture and gardens, while the grounds themselves reveal a series

Above: *The airy and shaded summer dining room, complete with elegant furnishings. Even the swallows find it agreeable, choosing to nest in a convenient corner.*

Right: *Shade-loving plants frame the rigorously composed view from the entrance lobby.*

of symmetrical courtyards. Mr Shoup borrowed the iconography of nineteenth-century urban architecture in Athens to create the house, and in doing so he brings to mind thoughts of a latter-day Harold Peto (though the latter drew on Italian precedent). Like Peto, Charles Shoup has long been a collector and rescuer of antiquities and interesting architectural salvage and, just as Peto had done in the Riviera, he used them to create a house and its garden in a seamlessly unified composition.

The gardens feature a dramatic sequence of courtyards and stairways, using local stone to build imposing architectural structures, such as pedimented gateways with fine decorative details and symmetrical niches wherein reside great urns or Classical statues. One of the most crucial things to get right from the start was the garden's water supply, and though the business of it is carefully hidden, the joy of water is celebrated everywhere, in pools, fountains and rills which carry its life-giving message throughout the gardens.

One particularly effective construction is an enclosed terrace, enjoying open views off to one side, but focusing on a series of steps leading through a reduced perspective of arches to a statue of Demeter, the earth mother or goddess of agriculture, framed by a shady grotto. The terrace itself is surfaced with a joyful arrangement of water-worn cobblestones picking out lunar patterns and contrasting pavings of limestone flags and terracotta bricks.

One of the reasons this house fits so well into its landscape is because natural and local materials have been used throughout. The same is true of the gardens: native olive trees provide the silvery-green frame-work around which other drought-tolerant plants of the Mediterranean have been used. Fragrant evergreen rosemary forms the crisp-edged hedges, and silver-green 'lawns' either side of a Doric portico have been

Above: *Handsome Cretan oil jars with their distinctive ribbed outline are placed at regular intervals along the axes of the garden; they also mark the ends of a simple seat, from where glorious views of the bay can be enjoyed.*

Left: *Young olive trees begin to form a tunnel, increasing the focus on the statue at the end of the vista. Extensive irrigation has enabled the plantings to flourish.*

fashioned out of close-clipped santolina. Dark-leaved acanthus fill out shady corners, while the European fan-palm of these southern shores – *Chamaerops humilis* – brings a quietly exotic air to the design. There are pots of fragrant-leaved pelargoniums, wayward hummocks of oleander and drowsy wands of white roses, which scramble into the olives and over pedimented gateways.

The ordered Classicism is tempered with lively decoration, both outdoors and among the interiors. Ranged on the terraces beside the house are numerous assorted clay pots for dramatic seasonal plants such as blue agapanthus, tumbling bougainvillea and diminutive herbs, while the drawing room in the north-east Pavilion Room was filled by Mr Shoup with an eclectic range of furnishings. Its Turkish kilims and inlaid tables, tapestries, deep sofas draped in colourful fabrics, vases, French and English furniture and carefully stowed books reveal that comfort and nurture have not been jettisoned in the pursuit of great style and perfection.

When the architectural historian David Watkin stayed at Cavogallo, he admired its fabulously conceived architectural plan and details, of course, but also another aspect which is difficult to capture adequately in photographs – the magic of the place after dark. 'Mr Shoup has devised a subtle lighting scheme which makes a night-time visit to the garden an unforgettable experience,' he wrote. Watkin also summed up Mr Shoup's Neo-Classical and Romantic inspirations: 'The tree-filled court at the heart of Cavogallo, swathed with vines, dotted with sculptural fragments and containing vistas through open porticoes, is immediately reminiscent of early-nineteenth-century buildings by Schinkel, such as Schloss Charlottenhof, near Potsdam, and of his unexecuted dream project, Schloss Orianda in the Crimea, overlooking the Black Sea. Mr Shoup has, indeed, made a dream come true by forging a further link in the chain connecting Pliny's descriptions of his villas with the visionary re-creations of them by Schinkel.'

Above: *Tiles, bricks and water-worn pebbles form textured and patterned paving in front of a pool. The statue of Demeter at the end of the vista marks the termination of the long north–south axis of the garden, with the goddess presiding over the fertility of the domain.*

Right: *Further down the long vista, a spreading holm oak brings character and shade to a cool area surrounding an antique marble fountain.*

'What is the name of this flower?' said I to Gioia.

She took the flower from my hand, looked at it lovingly and said: 'Fiore!'

'And what is the name of this one?'

She looked at it with the same tender attention and said: 'Fiore!'

'And how do you call this one?'

'Fiore! Bello! Bello!'

She picked a bunch of fragrant myrtle, but would not give it to me. She said the flowers were for S. Costanzo, the patron saint of Capri who was all of solid silver and had done so many miracles, S. Costanzo, bello! bello!

Axel Munthe, *The Story of San Michele*

Italy

Small-leaved and intertwining Ficus pumila *forms bizarre patterns around the columns of the loggia, which dominates the panoramic terraced garden.*

VILLA DEL BALBIANELLO, LAKE COMO

Viewed from the air, Villa del Balbianello on the western shore of Lake Como suggests the model village of a fairy tale, ranged along the tip of a wooded promontory. You expect that at any moment clockwork toy soldiers will march across the broad terrace of its ramparts – a fantasy given credence when you discover at close quarters the wheeled cannon on display in gardens of fantastical topiary.

It is a heart-wrenchingly romantic location, rising out of the reflective, deep waters of Como, with distant views of *alta Lombardia* and the famously scenic Engadine valley. Consequently, Balbianello has been a magnet for poets and artists for centuries, particularly during the Romantic period of the early nineteenth century.

The villa itself incorporates the vestiges of an ancient Franciscan convent, including a twin-towered chapel; though little is known about its history, Capuchin friars were still resident there in the sixteenth century. But it was not until Cardinal Angelo Maria Durini acquired the splendid estate of the Villa Balbiano in 1787 that its diminutive namesake, Balbianello, came into being. A cultured and worldly man,

Cardinal Durini chose the remote headland of Dosso d'Avedo for its air of solitude: in the spirit of the age, it provided the perfect place for quiet reading, meditations and literary discussions with his friends.

Arrival at Balbianello was – and still is – by boat, carefully steered into its tiny, statue-guarded harbour. From there the route is up a steep flight of steps, where you can pause to catch your breath (and the lake views) at one of the stairside balconies leaning out over the water. Cardinal Durini built his villa in three parts. The lowest section embraces the remains of the chapel; a square villa block occupies the middle terrace; and its upper storey looks across to Balbianello's most distinctive and attractive building: a loggia straddling the hilltop, taking in both southerly and northerly views over the lake.

Above: *The view from the lake: Balbianello's cypress and plane trees single it out as somewhere special, perched high on its promontory.*

Right: *Elegant carved balustrades line the terraces and frame glorious views of the mountains and lake. Owing to its location and relative isolation, Balbianello became a magnet for poets and artists, especially in the early nineteenth century.*

The garden's layout is also mainly Cardinal Durini's composition, though it was restored and enhanced in the 1970s by the property's last private owner, the explorer and mountaineer Count Monzino, and Italian landscape architect Emilio Trabella. By this late stage in its history, Balbianello had changed hands and fortunes several times, but it is easy to see the appeal that the location had for Monzino, with its steep, rocky terrain and alpine vistas.

Part of the fascination of Balbianello is that it is utterly unlike any other Italian garden. The topography ensured there was too little space to lay out the usual run of formal grounds; and in such a location flower gardens would have seemed irrelevant when the surrounding scenery is so overpowering. Instead, it is a symphony of greenery and carefully composed spaces, where you can take a variety of walks, either on the sunny south side among plane trees and agaves, or on the cooler, north-facing slopes with their tougher, alpine flora. Meanwhile, the various lake views are scrupulously maintained, with all the diverse trees and shrubs kept in check by careful pruning and training. In fact, for keen gardeners, the variety of topiary skills demonstrated here is quite as interesting as anything else about the place.

Small-leaved *Ficus pumila* crawls over the central columns of the loggia in crazy filigree patterns; it also forms a green waistcoat around the trunks of some of the trees and highlights architectural details such as balustrades and gateposts. Pruned ivy makes decorative swags here and there, and tiny-leaved *Muehlenbeckia complexa* is trimmed closely against the bases of lampposts. Closely packed-in bay bushes form a dark-green 'lawn' cascading over some of the steeper terrain (the gardeners clip them by hand, via a network of paths under the bushes' canopy). Where the bays grow in particularly precipitous positions, overhanging 30-foot-deep chasms, the writer Patricia Cleveland-Peck observed, 'They place their ladders against the rocks below and climb up through the shrubs until their heads and shoulders emerge through

Above: *Spiky leaves of* Agave americana *'Marginata' echo the little spires of what remains of the twin-towered chapel of a former Franciscan convent.*

Right: *Beyond the stooping branches of an old cedar, pruned plane trees line the path. The steep slope is covered with closely packed bay bushes – a challenge for the gardeners to cut back.*

unobtrusive holes from where they can clip as far as they can reach, repeating the process until the whole surface is covered.' Between November and January, clipping is concentrated on a huge holm oak in the private garden, when the gardeners tie themselves into the tree canopy and clip away by hand to maintain a smooth outline and uninterrupted lake views.

Since 1988, when Count Monzino died, Villa del Balbianello has been in the portfolio of Fondo per l'Ambiente Italiano (FAI). The count had bequeathed to the organisation not only the wonderful villa and its surrounding woods, but also its furniture, art collections, library and archives, plus a substantial endowment to enable Balbianello and his personal interests to reach a wider audience – a museum of mountaineering and polar expeditions fills one floor of the villa. The last word should be left to Monzino, who requested that the Italian flag be permanently hoisted over the jetty, 'in memory of all the flags my Alpine guides flew in many parts of the world, in a spirit of idealism, with humility but always with heroism'.

Above: *A path winds above the landing stage and the steep steps up to the garden.*

Right: *The attractive loggia takes in views both north and southwards over the lake.*

Left: *The view down to the lake shows the precipitous promontory on which the garden was built. The 'eiderdown' of bay trees is shown in the process of being pruned.*

LA MORTELLA, ISCHIA

Cast away at sea on the west coast of Ischia, an island fashioned out of violent volcanic eruptions, the garden of La Mortella (the myrtle) was laid out by the twentieth-century English composer Sir William Walton (1902–83) and his energetic Argentinian wife, Susana. It lies on the formidably steep and rocky south-facing slope of Monte Zaro, a challenging site by any standards, but one that the Waltons tackled with relish from 1956 onwards – even before building their home, which is also tucked into the rugged cliff-face.

Sir Laurence Olivier, their close friend for many years, counselled the Waltons against buying their chosen plot of land, advising them that it was 'nothing but a stone quarry' – but, fortunately, to no avail. A gently sloping gully below the hill was designated the garden area, with the house to be built in the lava rocks above it. 'The place drew us like a magnet. The shattering convulsion of nature's forces, which had wrested this landscape from the bowels of the earth, held us mesmerised,' wrote Lady Walton in her biography of the garden.

From the start they enlisted the landscape designer Russell Page, then at the height of his career, to design a garden among the stones;

his deceptively simple plan set the template for what Lady Walton accurately describes as an 'exotic split-level rock garden'. And exotic it certainly is, with luxuriant plantings of alocasias, vrieseas, epiphytic orchids, cycads and tree ferns.

From the entrance, down a little street leading off the main road which encircles the island, a curving path leads into the green canopies of pines and cypress trees, camellias and magnolias. And all at once the sound of water is audible in this gently musical garden, from several fountains and a flowing rill, accompanied always by birdsong. Water is so much an integral part of the garden that it is surprising to learn it was brought in only after much else had already been completed. This was because Ischia had access to precious little fresh water until a pipeline was laid under the sea from Naples in the late 1960s.

Right: In the lower garden, Russell Page made a Moorish-inspired fountain and rill to provide musical sounds of running water, joined by broad-leaved colocasias.

Below: In the upper gardens, a fire-break reservoir doubles as a water-lily pool, with a friendly-looking crocodile poised to dive into the water.

On such terrain, there is little choice but to go with the flow of the land. So Page's design, and Lady Walton's inspired extensions to the garden, follow an informal, winding ascent up the hillside, moving from the lush tropics of cyatheas hung with staghorn ferns, trailing tillandsias and bromeliads at the lower levels, through succulent agaves, spiky yuccas and puyas, cordylines and *Nolina recurvata*, to the dry rockfaces and contrastingly refreshing pools among holm oaks at the summit.

A network of water sprayers, mounted on tall, slender pipes, ensures that there is enough humidity for the tropical rainforest effect to be achieved within the gully. And it is at this lower level that you find the glass enclosure of the Victoria House, which maintains enough humidity to nurture a pool of *Victoria amazonica* water lilies, with their huge trays of leaves, overhung by brilliant orchids. The pool is backed by a carved mask face by Simon Verity, inspired by John Piper's theatrical curtain for *Façade,* an Edith Sitwell recital set to music by Walton early in his career. Bird sculptures, representing muses, appear through the gardens, and Verity carved a bird in flight just above the mask face, as though it were speaking into the artist's ear.

Continuing upwards through the garden, you might hear the strains of song or piano, wafting from the Fondazione William Walton – a study centre-cum-recital room for gifted young musicians and singers who attend masterclasses given by leaders in the field of music and opera. This is part of a cluster of buildings at the heart of the garden, which includes the composer's music room, the main house, a museum displaying Cecil Beaton's photographs of the composer and his friends, an orchid house with hummingbirds brought from Peru, and a stylish indoor/outdoor café shaded by large bamboo umbrellas.

Further ascents lead, via the canopies of tenacious olive trees and a stone archway, to William's Rock – a large, natural pyramid of basalt with spectacular views of the sea and distant Forio. Sir William Walton's ashes are placed within the stone, 'which he declared was his stone, on the day we bought the land,' Lady Walton says. Beyond it, a choice of paths wind along the cliff to the Nymphaeum Cannocchiale – a tiny, four-square courtyard with evergreen arbours enclosing ironwork seats set around a central modern fountain.

The garden has many intimate incidents, although others are less formally arranged, and part of the pleasure of exploration is coming across unexpected sitting areas for quiet contemplation or gazing out to sea. Everything is well labelled and the astonishingly rich plant collections amount to more than a thousand different species and varieties, including many rarities and plants now extinct in their wild habitats.

The top of the garden holds yet more surprises, with a fire-break reservoir disguised as a water-lily pool, presided over by a striking stone crocodile poised to dive in from a naturalistic cascade of rocks. The water winds round the top corner of the garden to the Thai Sala, a summerhouse hung with wind chimes overlooking a pool of magnificent sacred lotus, *Nelumbo nucifera,* a plant exquisite in leaf, flower and seedpod.

'For me, the garden is terribly important,' Lady Walton says. 'It embodies William; he lived for three decades here and composed his most beautiful music. The place is imbued with his spirit, with his music, and everybody who knows it considered that his cello concerto, in particular, contains the spirit of the place.' Undoubtedly, the garden is also permeated with Susana Walton's spirit, for her artistic eye and uncompromising influence is evident everywhere, from the archway entrance at the foot of the hill to the volcanic summit with its shingle-roofed meditation temple and dazzling lotus flowers.

Lady Walton has been the driving force not only behind the garden's creation and development but also in bringing it to the wider attention of potential visitors from overseas. In this respect, she has been quite as original as her garden and a tireless ambassador for the William Walton Foundation. Few who met her during her début at the Chelsea Flower Show in 2000, when she was displaying an exhibit based on La Mortella, including a remarkable collection of carnivorous plants, will forget her wonderful hat. Designed by the master hatter Philip Treacy, it was an evocation of the extraordinary multi-petalled flower of the *Victoria amazonica* water lily – like its wearer and its wearer's garden, exotic, extrovert, and something that brought pleasure to many.

Above: *One of La Mortella's most glamorous and reliable flowers, South African* Bauhinia galpinii, *located near the crocodile pool.*

Left: *In the steamy warmth of the Victoria House, a carved mask by Simon Verity was inspired by John Piper's theatre curtain for Walton's* Façade. *It overlooks rare* Victoria amazonica *water lilies.*

SANTA CHIARA, NAPLES

The spectre of Mount Vesuvius, one of the world's most dangerous volcanoes, looms over the frantic city of Naples. For more than sixty years it has sat quiet, apart from occasional cigar-like puffs released from its molten depths. Life in the city below, however, is lived in the fast lane – except, of course, when the congested traffic in its narrow streets shuffles along slower than a Neapolitan puppet-maker's arthritic grandmother.

Anthony Blunt, the art historian (and spy), described the city and its wonderful Baroque architecture as being 'like its inhabitants: lively, colourful, and with a tendency not to keep the rules, or rather, to have its own rules ...'. It is a widely accepted sentiment and certainly part of the allure of the place. When Father Giuseppe Reale, superior of the Santa Chiara monastery, was interviewed for *Country Life* in 2004, he explained the city's ambiguity: 'This is Naples: a city of colours, sounds, music. It's very religious but also very pagan, a place where myth and rationalism go hand in hand.'

And so there is no incongruity in the lively and generally secular decoration of the famous majolica tiles that decorate the pergola piers and low walls of the remarkable Santa Chiara cloister, hidden away in the heart of the old city. Here are hand-painted depictions of burgeoning grapevines ready for the wine press; scenes of village fêtes and revelry, of hunting, sea traders, a game of bowls, and – somewhat more in tune with Franciscan ideals – a nun feeding morsels of fish to grateful skinny cats.

The monastery of Santa Chiara was founded in the fourteenth century by Queen Sancia of Majorca, who provided for two enclosed orders, one being the monastery of Franciscan friars, and the other their female Franciscan counterpart, the Poor Clares order of nuns. 'The Clarissan convent centred on a huge but austere cloister, which served its purpose well until the eighteenth century, when its Gothic archi-tecture must have appeared positively drab to eyes more used to the magnificence of late Baroque and Rococo art,' observed the Italian writer Carla Passino. 'By then, Santa Chiara was the richest monastery in Naples, attracting scions of the finest families, and enjoyed the patronage of Queen Maria Amalia.'

In 1739, the Abbess Ippolita Carmignano had the inspired notion of engaging the respected Neapolitan architect, Domenico Antonio Vaccaro, to create a garden at Santa Chiara better suited to 'the decorum of noble ladies', where they could stroll comfortably on the clay paths they routinely trod and where 'walking and running would be comfortable and much more delightful'. In the succeeding years, much of Vaccaro's detail has been lost, including his intended plans for the flowerbeds, which would have been intensively gardened, especially with useful and medicinal herbs. Yet the basic four-square plan, with further four-square subdivisions and a central octagonal focus, has been

A view along the cloister of the monastery of Santa Chiara. Much of its beauty was destroyed by bombs in the Second World War, though careful restorations are now underway.

restored and Santa Chiara's exuberant majolica tilework, unique among monastic buildings of any period, is returning to its original form in substantial areas.

The commission for the tilework was given to the leading Neapolitan majolists of the eighteenth century, Donato and Guiseppe Massa, a father-and-son team, who covered each of the seventy-two octagonal piers of the pergolas with tiled scenes depicting extravagant garlands of grapevines. Bench seats linking each of those piers and several fountains were also highly decorated with fabulous cornucopias of flowers and fruits and with sixty-four rustic landscape scenes.

According to Father Reale, Vaccaro's garden provided the perfect setting for the madrigals and plays, minuets and balls that Abbess Carmignano staged during her tenure, but, since only royalty and courtiers were ever invited to Santa Chiara, the existence of a fabulous garden concealed in the very heart of Naples persisted as rumour rather than fact among the general population: 'It was not until 1924 – when the ever-shrinking number of novices led the Clarissan nuns to exchange convents with the neighbouring Franciscan friars – that the cloister was finally revealed to the city and started breathing the life of Neapolitan salons, attracting intellectuals of the calibre of [philosopher] Benedetto Croce.'

It was not long after this revelation that *Country Life* first published its remarkable photographs of the cloister, in 1928, when the drama of the composition could really be savoured, for at that time it was 'in a perfect state of preservation' and there were still real grapevines spreading luxuriant summer foliage along the cross beams, providing an alluringly umbrageous walk for spiritual contemplation.

Even so, it was to be another half-century before the garden was opened to the public in the 1970s, and restoration of the tilework, which had perished in the twentieth century, was carried out between 1987 and 2000. The process has not been easy, not least because wartime bombings in 1943 destroyed the monastery's archives, but a local landscaping company has worked hard to recreate the spirit of the place with appropriate plantings – of citrus trees, vines, aromatic herbs and box-edged beds. Santa Chiara still continues to be in the care of the Franciscan friars, and its future as a place of congregation, activity and interaction will endure.

Right: A detail of one of the bench backs, depicting rural revelry.

Below: Neapolitan majolica production peaked in the eighteenth century, when there was great demand for glazed vases, drug jars and tiles. Fabbrica Massa, the leading craftsmen, made Santa Chiara's famous tiled court (shown in its undamaged state on page 8).

VILLA DORIA PAMPHILJ, ROME

Olimpia Pamphilj, the central figure in the story of this exemplary villa garden in the south-west of Rome, was described by Evelyn March Phillipps a century ago as 'one of those strange personalities which stands out from the past in a vignette and creates an impression fresh and still vivid even after the lapse of more than two hundred years'. Certainly, her legacy is remarkable.

Olimpia Maidalchini was born at Viterbo, 50 miles north of Rome, in 1594 and, after being confined in a convent against her wishes (she was only released after accusing her confessors, perhaps falsely, of attempting to seduce her), she married a local nobleman. Thus began her dramatic ascent up the social ladder. But, soon after, her husband died and so did their infant son, leaving twenty-year-old Olimpia free to marry Pamfilio Pamphilj, a soldier and scion of an ascendant family, thirty years her senior.

Left: The great terrace viewed in detail shows a nineteenth-century taste for bedded-out flowers crammed into numerous dwarf-hedged beds. Potted lemon trees stand on elegant plinths, while palm trees reflect the vogue for exotic plants.

Below: Part of the magnificent Theatre Garden, overhung with mighty holm oaks.

Although he treated her unkindly, she had three sons by him, and meanwhile cultivated favour with his brother, the abbot Giovanni Battista, who was gaining influence in Vatican circles. Pamfilio died in 1639 and his brother was elected Pope Innocent X (an appointment that was also to make him the subject of Velázquez's most famous portrait) in 1644, by which time Olimpia had made herself indispensable to him. Famously avaricious and ostentatious, with unlimited ambition for herself and her sons, Olimpia financed the creation of a fine villa and lavish gardens for her son, Camillo, which are shown still reasonably intact in these shimmeringly atmospheric 100-year-old photographs taken by Charles Latham.

In 1630, Pamfilio Pamphilj had purchased a vineyard together with a modest house beside the Via Aurelia Antica, a short ride south from the Vatican. This plot of land was greatly extended by the acquisition of contiguous land after Pamfilio's brother had become Pope and a magnificent new villa, known as the Casino del Bel Respiro, was built on its hilltop. 'In one direction the eye travels over the wide campagna to where Monte Cavo, with its flat top, the site of the ancient temple of

Jupiter Latiarius, towers above the range of the Alban hills, while, looking in the opposite direction, there is such a view of St Peter's as can be obtained from no other point,' observed Evelyn March Phillipps. It was also an important site in itself, overlying the ancient gardens and tomb of the Emperor Galba (who died in AD 69), and believed to include more than thirty-four Classic tombs of great beauty.

Bernini came up with a fantastical scheme for the grounds of which the late Luigi Berliocchi, a garden historian who made a special study of the Doria Pamphilj properties, noted, '[it] provided for the building of walkways edged by parapets for strolls or, if there were floods, for the passage of small boats. He added an enormous Noah's Ark for living exotic beasts as well as sculpted and painted ones.'

All of this was not to Camillo Pamphilj's taste, however, and he chose instead the architects Alessandro Algardi and Giovan Francesco Grimaldi ('Il Bolognese') to lay out the grounds in the latest Baroque taste. Adjoining the villa on its garden front, the Secret Garden was laid out in formal style on that terrace, with geometrical flowerbeds, fountains and basins, salvaged Roman statues and new sculptures and regularly placed vases containing citrus trees. A centrally aligned double staircase led down from it, the two arms of the stairways framing a fountain of Venus, beyond which lay the spectacular Theatre Garden, a lavish example of a Roman Baroque garden with flowerbeds drawn

Top: *The front entrance of the mid-seventeenth-century Casino del Bel Respiro, photographed c.1900. It was built on a hilltop in the Trastevere district of south-west Rome.*

Above: *The magnificent Cascade Terrace in the park. Today it is hardly recognisable, as it has been vandalised and lacks any statuary, though water still flows through the fountain, down further cascades, and into the stream running through the park.*

Left: *The fountain of the Cascade Terrace seen close up, terminating a parkland vista.*

in sinuous curves, all enclosed by perimeter hedges with enormous amphorae placed at the corners.

Luigi Berliocchi's description of the gardens is illuminating: 'A large semicircular exedra, apparently inspired by the one in the Villa Aldobrandini in Frascati, ornamented with Classical sculptures, busts and bas reliefs, embraced this part of the garden. From this, two lateral wings spread out, each composed of eighteen small fountains, decorated with masks and shells, recalling the series of a hundred fountains in the Villa d'Este at Tivoli, and the Villa Ludovisi in Frascati. These wings were interrupted in the centre, and a nymphaeum was placed there, enclosed within a deep "rustic" grotto. At the centre of the exedra itself was a sculpture showing a faun engaged in playing his own musical repertory, the notes of which were produced by a water organ hidden behind his back. The intention was to call the attention of visitors who, as they drew near, would be sprayed by the gentle jets of water. The great park which surrounded the Theatre Garden included long avenues of ilexes, laurel copses, orchards, a deer park, a hunting reserve, many bird nets and a stream which ran through a series of little waterfalls.'

This arrangement was unaltered for a century-and-a-half, until the English landscape style, increasingly in vogue throughout Europe,

spread through Roman gardens like a rash in the second half of the eighteenth century, under the modernising influence of Francesco Bettini. Even so, the Theatre Garden, with its musical fountains and grottoes, survived intact until 1848, whereupon the garden was all but destroyed during the Siege of Rome.

Subsequent restoration of the grounds was minimal, and while the structural features were retained where possible, nineteenth-century taste favoured the planting of exotic trees, such as palms and cedars, into vast lawns. In the late twentieth century, things got worse for the vast park when a dual-carriageway road was driven through the middle of it, forever separating it in two.

Today, the villa and its Secret Garden are also kept aloof from the rest of the grounds, well maintained but reserved for government use, such as receptions and international summits. Meanwhile, there are vestiges of the Theatre Garden which, with the broader park, comprise a valuable but surprisingly under-funded public amenity.

Above: *The parterre on the great terrace, as photographed by Charles Latham c.1900. Today its dwarf hedges have thickened into bold, swirly patterns, filling up the spaces where the flowers and gravels used to be.*

Right: *A view of the 'English' park of irregular lawns and specimen trees, set out below the formal terrace. A nineteenth-century taste for exotic trees was indulged.*

VILLA HANBURY, VENTIMIGLIA

In its day, through the last third of the nineteenth century and the first half of the twentieth, La Mortola (also known as the Villa Hanbury) nurtured one of the greatest botanical collections in the world in deftly laid-out gardens on an exquisite stretch of coast. Its greatness was due to the collaboration of two gifted and wealthy brothers – Sir Thomas Hanbury (1832–1907), pioneer businessman in China and Quaker philanthropist, and his eldest brother, Daniel (1825–75), a chemist and botanist with widespread connections throughout the botanical world.

These black and white pictures reveal the gardens as they were in 1928, mature and in the hands of the next generation, but for decades La Mortola had already been a mecca for all lovers of plants and Mediterranean gardens, receiving even in Edwardian times more than 5,000 garden visitors per year. The limestone hills of the Menton range protected the burgeoning collections from cold winds sweeping off the Alps to the north, and the benign situation – beside the sea and close to Menton – was considered to be the most horticulturally favourable on the Riviera.

When Sir Thomas Hanbury first saw La Mortola, in 1867, he viewed it from a boat; at that time the railway only went as far as Nice, and journeys farther east had to be made by the uncomfortable horse-drawn diligence coach on the old and winding Corniche road, or by sea. His brother Daniel had actually discovered it three years earlier and immediately realised its potential for the creation of a botanical garden, but he needed to get his wealthy brother interested in the proposition. Closer inspection revealed that the formerly elegant Palazzo Orengo was being used as a farm occupied by an old peasant and his wife, its dining room a stable for mules and the hallway blocked with oil jars and barrels of wine, while bats and swallows had free range in the *salons* of the *piano nobile*.

Right: *An inclining tree provides sturdy support for rampant climbers, framing a view of the villa. The very steep nature of the site provides countless viewpoints, especially of the Villa Hanbury, the former Palazzo Orengo.*

Below: *Thriving in dry soil on the top of a rock wall, the succulent leaf rosettes and pink flower sprays of* Aloe hanburyana. *Aloes are well represented in the gardens.*

Sir Thomas's acquisition of the property and its surrounding olive groves in 1868 led to a turnaround in the fortunes of the villa, which he employed local craftsmen to restore and sensitively extend, simultaneously creating stairways and scenic walks through the growing botanical collections in the gardens. Nurtured in the Riviera sunshine and in soil made fertile with manure and water, the imported seedlings of acacia, yucca, pittosporum and eucalyptus, plus young palm trees in variety, filled out into mini-forests. Huge ranges of succulents found footings in the rocky slopes and climbing plants in great variety were draped over pergola walks and balustrades.

Dr J. Henry Bennet, a local physician, and a contemporary and friend of Sir Thomas, explained in great detail in *Winter and Spring on the Shores of the Mediterranean* why Menton and its environs were the best location for aiding and even curing consumptives. Those benefits also happened to suit the widest range of plants: 'One important reason why the climate of Menton and the Riviera is beneficial ... is that it is seldom or never, at the same time, *cold and wet*,' Dr Bennet wrote. 'When the

weather is cold, it is with north winds, and the air is dry. When the air is moist, south winds prevail, and the temperature is mild.'

Though it was certainly a plantsman's garden – crammed with echiums, aeoniums, palms and argyranthemums from the Canary Islands, and wisterias, species clematis and roses brought directly from the Far East – La Mortola later acquired a more consciously designed landscape, although one that lacked Renaissance rigour. It already had the benefit of a mature cypress avenue – a survivor of the villa's glory days – and spectacular views from its levelled-out upper terraces.

Further walks were added, including the New Vista, a long, straight walk with intervals of steps, leading down to an intact stretch of the Via Aurelia, the ancient road linking Italy and Gaul, through which Napoleon and his army also travelled in 1796. The Via Aurelia, an atmospheric little thoroughfare bordered by high, medieval walls, cut through the lower gardens, but beyond it, accessed by a bridge, La Mortola's domain extended right down to where the sea breaks on to a pebbly beach, and this low point was the location for its kitchen garden.

In 1928, Cecil Hanbury (1871–1937), Sir Thomas's son, confirmed that the importance of La Mortola as a hub for botanical excellence and research was being maintained in the next generation: 'About 12,000

Above: *The former Palazzo Orengo, viewed through scarlet aloes and mature cypress trees lining one of the paths zigzagging up the steep hill to the road at the top.*

Left: *A detail of the lookout point on the main terrace, framed by spiny aloes.*

packets of seeds are distributed every year gratis to botanic gardens and private individuals all over the world, and many interesting seeds and plants are received in exchange.' Although the gardens had become neglected during the First World War years, Cecil Hanbury and his wife, Dorothy, reinvested in La Mortola. Impressed by the coherence of design they had seen at Harold Peto's Villa Maryland (*see page 72*) on Cap Ferrat, they reshaped La Mortola's formerly wiggly paths into long vistas and capitalised on its fine views, introducing seats, formal pools and eye-catching statuary.

After Cecil's death in 1937, Dorothy Hanbury stayed at La Mortola throughout the Second World War and the property continued in Hanbury family ownership until 1962, when it was ceded to the Italian state. Today, the gardens with their lofty palms and soaring cypresses are managed by the University of Genoa and the salmon-pink-washed Palazzo Orengo is used by the administrative staff. Although there is still much work to be done to refurbish a garden that for decades in the twentieth century lacked enough staff, it remains, due to its location, topography and Romantic history, one of the most inspiring and unselfconsciously ravishing gardens of the world.

Above: *An interior photograph of the villa reveals some of the Oriental furniture and* objets d'art *that the Hanburys brought back in quantity from the Far East.*

Left: *The terrace, south of the house, takes in sea views, framed by elegant pines and palms.*

SANT'ANTONIO, TIVOLI

'Garden and orchard must be very close to home – the garden best of all lying below the byre, whose liquid feed will of its own accord fertilise it,' advised Palladius, the fourth-century author of *Work of Agriculture*. This advice seems to have been taken up at some stage at the property that later became known as Sant' Antonio. In the dark ages, this former Roman villa became a working farm and the remarkable first-century BC grotto attached to it was used as a cow barn, located above terraced gardens descending the steep hillside.

Sant' Antonio can be considered in relation to the Villa Gregoriana (*see page 166*), for these two properties face each other across the scenic chasms of the Aniene River. But whereas the Villa Gregoriana is a Romantic, 'natural' wooded landscape, watery and shaded, Sant' Antonio has long been a cultivated area on an open, south-facing hillside.

The original Roman name for the Sant' Antonio villa is lost in the mists of time, but it is one of a great many residences of the Republican and Imperial era that were scattered all over the hills around Tivoli and into the plain below. Though its land has always been cultivated, the terraced gardens are believed to be medieval, since the property became a monastic house in the thirteenth century. According to the architec-

tural historian Richard Haslam, who pieced together a brief and fascinating history of the property, the Roman villa at Sant' Antonio 'stood largely intact until 1583 ... it then served as a residence and monastery of St Francis's third order of friars, or Order of Penitence ... No doubt a chapel was set up in their house, and later dedicated to St Francis's contemporary St Anthony of Padua, from which the name of its successor was derived.'

Above: *The modest entrance to the church of Sant' Antonio. The great waterfall of the Villa Gregoriana can be seen in the distance.*

Right: *The villa of Sant' Antonio, dating back to Roman times, viewed from the terrace of the lower garden, framed by olive trees.*

When, in 1461, Pope Pius II built the Rocca Pia, a massive fortress at the southern end of old Tivoli, erected to frown menacingly over the quarrelsome and proud local population, he stayed for three months at Sant' Antonio to oversee the works, but his sojourn was far from comfortable, as he fulminated in his diary: 'The house was old and tumble-down, full of rats as big as rabbits, which disturbed the night with their scuttling up and down. The winds too, of which the city has great wealth, were annoying and it was impossible to keep the rain out of the leaky old building which the careless monks had not taken the trouble to repair.'

At some stage, rumour spread that in Roman times it had been the house of the Augustan poet Horace (65–8 BC), and this was one of the myths that encouraged eighteenth-century travellers on the Grand Tour to include Tivoli in their schedules. One such tourist, looking for an ideal spot from which to paint the famous waterfalls of Tivoli, was

Frederick Augustus Searle (1824–1902) who bought the wonderfully located Sant' Antonio.

From 1879, when he acquired Sant' Antonio, for the next quarter of a century, Searle restored the buildings, in the process finding the remains of the Roman grotto. Haslam has written that the Roman building 'began as a row of at least three separate, tall houses – similar to a number still standing in Tivoli – and was located above an earlier villa on the bluff. They were served by the Roman road which skirts the head of the valley and then follows it on the side facing the town for a mile or more of the finest views. The Hellenistic grotto was formed beneath one of these houses, and has a floor of fine, white mosaic, a shuttered vault of concrete spanning almost 35 ft, and a coffered niche built into the hillside.'

The grotto had originally enjoyed splendid views of Tivoli, but these were obscured by the terraces made for the medieval monastery garden, which appropriated them. The views are little changed today; the grounds still capture the flavour of a working garden of vines, olives, figs, other fruits and shrubby herbs that fill out the sun-filled terraces.

Searle's descendants continue to own Sant' Antonio, which is presently administered by the Landmark Trust as a glamorous property that can be rented out for short periods.

Overleaf: *A room with a view: Tivoli from Sant' Antonio* (left), *and the falls of the Villa Gregoriana* (right). *The two properties face each other across the chasms of the Aniene River.*

Left: *Bird's-eye view: the levelled-out terraces are believed to date from medieval times, created for the monastery garden in the thirteenth century.*

Below: *A scene of rustic productivity which may have changed little for many hundreds of years, except for the high-rise building on the opposite side of the valley.*

VILLA GREGORIANA, TIVOLI

On a tree-clad elbow of the Aniene River is a magnificent, anciently famous landscape of mysterious chasms, cascades of rushing water, green glades and genteelly grimy grottoes. This place is known as the Villa Gregoriana – though it is not the glamorous sort of villa in which the region of Lazio excels. Unlike its near-neighbour, the sixteenth-century Villa d'Este, with its frescoed *palazzo* frowning magnificently over tiers of statue-populated terraces and erupting fountains, Gregoriana is a villa in the earlier sense of the word, being a simple country property – a sacred grove beside a rustic farm.

It is not without drama, however, for this grove plunges dramatically down a cliff beside the narrow streets of Tivoli, in the Monti Tiburtini, 18 miles east of Rome. Old Tivoli, a crooked maze of little lanes perched hugger-mugger on a craggy plug of limestone, is hemmed in by Gregoriana's deep, tree-clad gorges on one side and the dark evergreens of the Villa d'Este terraces on the other. Around it the Aniene carves a tortuous path before it joins the meanders of the Tiber.

It was this dramatic combination of scenery, abundant water and travertine stone which made Tivoli into a fashionable spot for wealthy Romans to build their country villas, well over two millennia ago. Its Classical past can still be found piecemeal everywhere, though medieval and later constructions replaced what must have been a fascinating and complex town; as many as 350 Roman villas are believed to have been built in the neigh-bourhood, excluding those that are part of the complex of Emperor Hadrian's villa in the valley nearby.

The focal point for Tivoli is still its acropolis, supporting glamorous ruins – the round temple of Vesta and the rectangular temple of the Albunean Sibyl beside it. These structures, teetering on the edge of a steep gorge hung with trees and foaming with waterfalls, became icons of the Grand Tour. Consequently, many English landscape gardens of the eighteenth century boasted temples modelled on this powerfully Romantic template. The garden historian Christopher Thacker pointed out that Tivoli influenced painters and landscape gardeners in the eighteenth century more than any other single scene.

A catastrophic flash flood of the Aniene, which drains the fast-flowing waters off the surrounding hills, smashed through the old town in 1826. Many buildings, people and animals were mercilessly gathered and washed away in its awesome swell, but the tragedy did lead to one happier outcome: the creation of one of the most remarkable and

dramatic landscape parks in the western world, under the instruction of Pope Gregory XVI (1765–1846).

Gregory was renowned as a conservative in both politics and theology, continually at loggerheads with the views of liberals urging reform, but he was both pious and kind and showed a preference for simplicity. He did, however, spend lavishly on architectural and engineering works and the Villa Gregoriana landscape was one of his earliest undertakings as Pope. Under the direction of French engineers, a massive canal tunnel was cut through the rock of Monte Catillo, diverting the river away from the town. At its far end, the water was guided to the cliff edge to plunge in a 300-foot drop beyond the narrow neck of the valley, out of harm's way. It makes a compelling garden feature, creating a deafening roar when the sluices are wide open, reliably raising a mist and a perfect rainbow you can almost reach out and touch, from the terrifying 'horseshoe' platform nearby.

Whether you enter Villa Gregoriana from its gateway by the temples or from the opposite side, close to the Gregoriano Bridge which spans the gorge, a series of paths zigzag their way down in easy steps to the valley bottom. Expect to be amazed en route, as those on the Grand Tour were, by the rock formations of limestone; by the thunderous water that emerges here and there out of caverns and cascades; by the cool shade of the woods, dappled with cyclamen in spring; by ferns and fragrant wallflowers springing out of stony crevices. Then, about halfway down, there is the marvel of the Miollis Gallery, a walk-through tunnel with a series of triangular windows offering peephole views of the gorge and its mighty falls. It was created in 1809 and commemorates the French General Miollis, then Governor of Rome. And on the opposite cliff-face, somewhat concealed by trees, there is a villa after all – the crumbling ruins and vaulted chambers of the house of Manilius Vopiscus, a Roman Consul in AD 114.

The remarkable, and massive, restorations undertaken by Fondo per L'Ambiente Italiano (FAI) have ensured that today this magical land-scape is once again a priceless place of sanctuary.

Above: *The churned-up rock formations are a geological spectacle many come to see.*

Right: *The round Temple of Vesta and, beside it, the Temple of the Albunean Sibyl dominate the clifftop above the steep valley landscape known as the Villa Gregoriana.*

Overleaf: *The dramatic valley of the Aniene River. On the left-hand side, the old town of Tivoli sits above the great wooded chasm of the Villa Gregoriana.*

ISOLA MADRE, LAKE MAGGIORE

The shrill cries of peacocks provide an appropriate soundtrack for the gardens of Isola Madre. Like the island's imported palm trees, banana plants, camellias and hibiscus, peafowl are exotic creatures of the Far East. In the mythology of the Indian subcontinent, the peacock is ubiquitous; it symbolises, among other things, fertility, good luck, and the arrival of the monsoons. Near the western shore of Lake Maggiore, the Borromean Islands do not need to worry about monsoons, of course (though spring and summer rains are plentiful, owing to the proximity of the mountains); but their year-round mild climate – due to the lake's absorption and storage of summer heat, released from the water during the winter months – is the reason why Mediterranean and subtropical flora grow so well here.

Isola Madre, which covers 20 acres, is the largest of the Borromean Isles, which were named after the local landowning family of Borromeo, exiled from Tuscany in the fourteenth century, who have wielded considerable power in the locality of Maggiore since 1501. Initially, the island was made up of simple, roughly terraced farmland nurturing orchards and olive groves, with remnants of Roman occupation. With the arrival of the Borromeo family, the variety of produce was widened to include figs, mulberries, walnuts, grapevines, quinces, pomegranates and highly prized orange and lemon trees, among other edibles. Count Lancellotto Borromeo built a modest residence on the island in the early sixteenth century; it is easy to imagine the appeal that this place must have had, with its fertile land, a lake full of fish, a benevolent climate and misty mountain views. Before the century was out, his successor, Renato I Borromeo, built a substantial *palazzo* more in keeping with the family's ascendancy in the region.

Above: *On an upper terrace, spring blossoms are joined by a ribbon of dashing yellow pansies.*
Right: *Fragrant wisteria garlands an iron arcade straddling the great staircase. The treads of each stair are infilled with a surface of rounded pebbles.*

However, in the 1630s, the grandeur of Isola Madre was eclipsed by the massive constructions going on just a short distance across the water. Another relation, Count Carlo Borromeo, was building the magnificent Baroque palace and terraced gardens of Isola Bella, which were completed a generation later by his son, Count Vitaliano Borromeo.

The two islands are so different from one another that admirers of one are not always so keen on the other. William Brockedon (1787–1854), the painter, writer and inventor, regarded Isola Bella as an island 'worthy of the extravagance of a rich man with the taste of a confectioner', while Dorothy Wordsworth (1771–1855) considered its terraces, rockwork and shellwork 'the peak of absurdity, a garden not of flowers but of stones, where coloured pebbles take the place of flowers'. Versed in the English landscape movement and the Picturesque aesthetic, they could not think otherwise, and so Isola Madre held the key to English hearts.

Left: *Parts of the garden appear almost like an English park. The warty root growths of* Taxodium distichum *spring up like molehills in the lawn.*

Below: *Always ready for a photo opportunity, Isola Madre's white peacocks stand out dramatically against one of the garden's many brilliant azaleas.*

By 1905, Richard Bagot, author of the popular Edwardian guidebook *The Italian Lakes*, could offer the heaving numbers of British tourists filling the belle époque hotels of the lakeshores a more personal critique than they would find in Baedeker. 'The gardens [of Isola Bella] are a triumph of bad taste,' he wrote. 'Artificial grottos bristling with shells, terrible pieces of hewn stone, which it would be an offence to sculpture to term statuary, offend the eye at every turn. The vulgarity of the whole conception is redeemed by the luxuriance of the semi-tropical vegetation which, owing to the extreme mildness of the climate, flourishes in these islands, and by the beauty of the views across the lake, to be enjoyed from every angle of the terraces. ... The Isola Madre, on the contrary, which has never acquired the popularity possessed by its rococo neighbour, ... is eminently satisfactory.'

Bagot's assessment reflected a very English view of what gardens and scenery ought to contain. Isola Madre's rustic charm had been enhanced in the early nineteenth century by its transformation into a fashionable English-style landscape park. The plant collections expanded, too, through the nineteenth century, and the relative humidity supplied by the lake ensured that rhododendrons and azaleas could thrive beside verdant lawns, with camellias and exotic trees being imported to Europe from plant-hunters' expeditions in the Far East.

Of the garden's many fine specimen trees, several stand out for special mention. Standing back a little from the palm avenue, with its broad gravel walk, you cannot miss the Chilean palm (*Jubaea spectabilis*), a giant with a thick, muscular trunk and a fine symmetrical head of foliage, dwarfing all other palms in the vicinity. It was planted in 1858 and is now well over 60 feet tall. In a good year it is capable of producing more than 3,000 *coquitos* or tiny coconuts.

Isola Madre also boasts a massive *Cupressus cashmeriana* sheltered by the inner courtyard of the *palazzo*, which is known (incorrectly, as it turns out) as the Kashmir Court in its honour. This most graceful of conifers, with its pendulous tresses of dusky blue-green foliage, is very rare in the wild and actually comes from the remote and inaccessible countries of Bhutan and Arunachal Pradesh, though cultivated specimens occur around temples in Kashmir. Then there is the aromatic camphor tree, *Cinnamomum camphora* from China, which has matched the large proportions it generally achieves in the old gardens of the Riviera, and a huge *Cedrus atlantica*, the cedar of the Atlas Mountains of North Africa. With its wide-spreading arms of matt foliage, it provides a grand photo opportunity for visitors when the garden's famous white peacocks clamber on to its lower branches.

Whereas Isola Bella, in all its Rococo splendour, is nothing less than a spectacular floating theatre (literally, in fact, as theatrical performances were played out on its terraces in the seventeenth and eighteenth centuries, with musical choruses hidden in the gardens and apparently floating in the air, singing from boats along its shore), Isola Madre is a gentle spectacle, saving its most dramatic moment for rhododendron time each spring. Then, beneath the forest-like canopy of its tree collections, the azaleas and rhododendrons erupt into a multi-coloured frenzy of pinks, magentas, yellow, orange, white, pale rose, purple and primrose. Even then, it is difficult for the strange white peacocks to be upstaged, since they appear as a chorus of dancing girls (or cross-dressing ones, since the extravagant plumage is only on the males) in a particularly beautiful, if not exactly musical, cabaret.

Above: *Even from some distance, the garden's enormous Chilean palm,* Jubaea spectabilis, *creates a memorable landmark beside the villa.*

Right: *At closer quarters, the Chilean palm still dwarfs everything else around it. It was planted in 1858 and is now well over 60 feet tall.*

Our road in the evening lay between lofty slopes partially covered with bushes of rosemary and lavender in the fullest bloom. The sun went down behind the chain of hills which form the coast of the sea, just as we reached a quinta belonging to Forjaz, at present governor of Madeira. As we approached the rich cultivated plains framed in by the hills around Cadafaiz, we heard the country people, men, women, and children, singing hymns to Saint Anthony as they returned home from reaping.

William Beckford, *Recollections of an Excursion to the Monasteries of Alcobaça and Batalha*

Portugal

Detail of corsair ship embroidery at Flor da Rosa. Its theme, of captives aboard a Barbary corsair's vessel, was familiar to Portuguese seafarers in earlier centuries.

FLOR DA ROSA, ALGARVE

Portugal has a long tradition of grand country house gardens. Famous examples abound in the countryside around Lisbon and Oporto, as well as further inland near Coimbra. The Roman and Moorish influences that swept through Spain also fashioned Portugal's garden iconography – the colonnaded enclosures, formal box parterres, central fountains and decorative tilework all have common origins in the gardens of Spain and North Africa. Yet Portuguese gardens have a distinct heritage of their own, particularly in the use of *azulejos*, the decorative tiles that are frequently used to compose large, scenic compositions, and in fine topiary. Both of these elements reached a high point in, among other places, the eighteenth-century royal palace gardens of Queluz, west of Lisbon, where small boats sailed along a tiled canal.

Left: *The small, box-edged parterre, dominated by slender cypresses, makes a formal and welcoming setting for the converted farmhouse.*

Below: *A view down the cypress-lined drive with traditional cobble paving.*

But in the Algarve, in the extreme south, things are different. For geographical and cultural reasons, there is not the same tradition of palatial houses and gardens, but instead simple farmhouses (many now holiday homes) dot the interior, while much of the coast is a permanent building site of new hotels, apartments and cheek-by-jowl villas.

A fine example of a simple country farm sensitively converted into a residence is at Flor da Rosa, where we see a very different side to Portuguese garden-making: that of an elegantly restrained, private family villa, the sort that is never on the tourist itinerary, even though it is reasonably close to the popular Algarve coast. This particular garden has been made only since 1970. Vertical cypress trees were planted to line its drive, in the Tuscan manner, and other factors reinforce the sense that this garden could be in Italy – the warm yellow-ochre and terracotta colour washes on the walls, and the rendered buttresses pressing against the lower storey of the house, giving this small, carefully restored farmhouse the stature of a fortified dwelling.

Verticality is also emphasised by a line of poplars towering over an ivy-covered wall, where a niche displays a carved Roman centurion, thrown into elegant relief against his shroud of greenery.

The pavings are carefully thought out too, in the Portuguese way, with carefully laid cobblestones on the drive and fired bricks paving the formal garden paths. One might have been led to conclude that the property's name of Flor da Rosa derived from a preference for roses in the gardens, but that is not the case; its magic and serenity are achieved from its greenery rather than from flowers (of which there are few) and also from the carefully worked-out spaces, which work in harmony with the proportions of the house. The name, on the other hand, refers back in time to a monastery founded in the fourteenth century by an ancestor of the owner.

An entrance through a crenellated wall leads into the formal garden, which is exactly aligned on the south-facing elevation of the house. Set against the house walls are two bench seats under the ground-floor windows, of square outline and decorated with the tiles for which Portugal is so famous. Here we can see one of Portugal's Moorish influences brought into play: seats so boxy that even Le Corbusier would have admired them, but decorated with ornamental tiles that bring a sudden note of jollity into an otherwise austere composition. We have seen such benches already in this book, in the old Ottoman gardens of Algiers.

In the traditional manner inherited from Rome and from the Middle East, the formal garden reflects the symmetry of the house and sidles up against it, creating order in the proximity of a dwelling. A diminutive double stairway, perfectly aligned on the central doorway, leads down gently into the parterre garden, the risers of the steps prettily patterned with colourful stonework. At the parterre's centre, a small but elegant fountain forms the focal point for the composition; around it, the topiarised box plants echo both the great gardens of Portugal and also of Italy, so that again there is a sense of national boundaries blending and blurring.

Flor da Rosa is an elegant example of contemporary garden-making in the Mediterranean region, and, as such, it has the obligatory swimming pool. Set into a private courtyard enclosed by some of the service buildings of the farm, with their colour-washed walls, it is an inviting, serene and minimalist composition, with little decoration apart from a niche housing an elegant amphora, and some carefully positioned terracotta pots.

Old farm buildings were incorporated into an elegant courtyard for the swimming pool.
A pedimented niche was specially made to create a centrepiece, housing a slender amphora.
Otherwise, decoration is minimal, with plenty of space created for sunloungers.

CASA DA INSUA, BEIRA ALTA

Throughout the summer the biggest draw for visitors to Casa da Insua, in the rolling countryside of the Beira Alta province, is its ravishing garden, a brilliant jewel box set within a luxuriant broader landscape of orchards and vineyards. The house was built for Luis de Albuquerque (1739-97) the captain-general of the Brazilian province of Mato Grosso, who filled it with treasures from the Far East as well as artefacts from South America. The site is sheltered from the north by its woodland belt of magnificent trees – including cedars, oaks, eucalyptus, pines and cypresses, but looks out over sloping ground dropping away in productive platforms. Along the south front of the house, the gardens are formally laid out on two riotously colourful terraces, from which further paths lead eastwards into a Romantic 'English landscape' garden covering several acres.

Above: *Impressive box topiary in the formal gardens, with seasonal flowers infilling each bed of the fan-shaped design.*

Left: *The clipped camellias form larger hedging; on the far left, part of the camellia room with its central pool of lotus flowers can be seen.*

In 1909, the estate's then proprietor, Manuel de Albuquerque, wrote a brief description of the garden as it had been designed in the second half of the eighteenth century (the house was probably built around 1770–80). He noted the parterre of the terraces, its 'geometric outline ... All the flowerbeds are surrounded by box representing cornucopia, vases, fans, etc ... It is curious that this box has been clipped with all possible care every year since it was planted.'

Though Casa da Insua embraced the fashionable English landscape style that was sweeping through Europe, it clearly never came right up to the doors of the house, as it did in some other properties, since here the formal and woodland areas were laid out simultaneously, the formal leading decorously into the informal. Some of the low box hedges – particularly the coat-of-arms and fleur-de-lys designs close to the house – were renewed in 1930, but the beds beyond are much older. They are gaily filled with roses, marguerites and cannas, while brilliant bougainvillea and morning glory fasten themselves to the house walls.

Historians find it curious that Manuel de Albuquerque failed to mention the topiarised camellias that make such eye-catching and

splendid garden architecture today, and that must have achieved the same effect in his day. But Casa da Insua's topiarised camellia 'house' with various 'doorway' entrances cut into its sides is not so very unusual in historic Portuguese gardens. Perhaps it was not a feature he cared for; or maybe it was simply, as the historians have concluded, that Albuquerque believed the camellias of Insua not worthy of special comment. Nevertheless, today the camellia room of Insua is a great draw, admired not just for itself, but also for its central pool filled with *Nelumbo nucifera*, the sacred lotus flower, bearing remarkable glaucous foliage and sculptural seedheads.

Whether Albuquerque liked the camellias or not, the genus has a special relationship with Portuguese gardens as a whole. The family archives of the Conde de Campo Bello are said to have recorded at the Villa Nova de Gaya in Oporto three camellias being planted in the gardens in 1550. The camellia expert Jennifer Trehane says it 'seems a likely story, because the Portuguese were in Japan in 1542 when one of their ships was shipwrecked there, and there was certainly active trade between Japan and Portugal between 1549 and 1639'. However, Trehane concludes, 'the origin of [the Villa Nova] plants has been vigorously denied by historians and by family descendants, who claim that the first camellias were brought into the Oporto area between 1808 and 1810.' There has certainly been a tradition of camellia-growing in Portugal since at least the end of the seventeenth century, and by the late 1800s, Portuguese nurserymen were actively introducing new varieties. 'One nursery listed 665 varieties in his 1887 catalogue, 161 of them Portuguese bred,' according to Trehane.

Beyond the formal gardens of Casa da Insua, the mood becomes relaxed and playful, with numerous woodland walks, each avenue individually named with its own little sign. These lead the visitor to stroll into different glades, each boasting its own special features. One has fountains; another focuses on an altar and altarpiece; there is an island with stone seats and table; elsewhere are a basin inset with stone flowerbeds and a menagerie.

Back at the house, a pair of two-storey pavilions with arcaded loggias add an imposing weight to each end of the handsome white villa. Look above to the roof parapet and you notice that the pointed battlements decorating each pavilion are pierced with fleur-de-lys, the iris motif, which appears appropriate to the garden setting. However, Marcus Binney, who wrote a detailed account of Casa da Insua in 1984, points out that their raison d'être has historical and aspirational connotations rather than horticultural ones: 'These crenellations with pointed tops are a feature of certain Portuguese keeps of towers in the late Middle Ages or 16th and early 17th centuries ... introduced to give the house a deliberately backward look and sense of ancestry'.

Today, the house has achieved that cherished ambition of longevity, and is still owned by the family whose most famous ancestor was Alfonso de Albuquerque. The dominant figure in Portuguese India in the early sixteenth century, he captured Goa and turned it into the jewel of Portugal's eastern empire.

Left: *A still pool reflects the garden front of the house.*

They drove very slowly, looking out for a tree which would give them shade, for the late sun was slanting low across the fields, driving the shadows into patches far too thin for two men to sit in them at ease. Finally, under the ruined wall of an outhouse, which belonged to an abandoned farm, they found what they needed. Someone had painted a hammer and sickle crudely in red upon the crumbing stone.

'I would have preferred a cross,' Father Quixote said, 'to eat under.'

Graham Greene, *Monsignor Quixote*

Spain

The upper gallery of the Patio Grande, or central courtyard, with paintings of literary worthies, dating from 1539.

CASA DE PILATOS, SEVILLE

On the east side of old Seville, the Plaza de Pilatos is a handsome city square shaded by tall palm trees, brooded over by a statue of the painter Francisco de Zurbarán (1598–1664) with palette and paint-brushes to hand. From the square you can access one of the loveliest hidden buildings of Seville: the elegant Moorish-inspired palace of Don Fadrique Enríquez de Ribera (1476–1539), the 1st Marquis of Tarifa. A pious and wealthy Catholic nobleman, he took over the house, begun by his parents, in the 1520s and created the one that can be seen today.

It is interesting to reflect that the Casa de Pilatos is an exact contemporary of Cardinal Wolsey's creation Hampton Court, west of London beside the River Thames, though one cannot imagine either palace in the other's location. Whereas Hampton Court is an extrovert statement of power and grandeur set beside the river for all to see, Casa de Pilatos speaks of the Mediterranean and especially the introspective, private *Mudéjar* style, an inheritance that was readily adopted into Spanish architectural sensibilities with the reconquest of southern Spain.

The garden interest of Pilatos lies in its patios and the enclosed green courts beyond, which are among the most beautiful and well kept in Andalucía. The entrance or carriage courtyard is a serene, plain space with a grid pattern in its paving formed by contrasting light and dark stone cobbles. (At Casa Postigo, *see page 196*, the Spanish garden designer Fernando Caruncho employed this time-honoured device in a modern, minimalist concept in the front entrance area.) In the Moorish manner, the entrance to Casa de Pilatos is formal, understated and businesslike, contrasting with the hidden splendours to be explored beyond. Its edges are blurred, however, with cascades of vines and a great bougainvillea drenched in the magenta bracts that surround each of its thousands of flowers.

Through the arcaded loggia, so successfully curtained by the bougainvillea, lies the Patio Grande, the central courtyard where two storeys of arcades wrap around, overlooking a glamorous, marble-paved court with an Italian marble fountain at the centre. This courtyard is highly admired for its combination of architectural inspiration and fragments from the Roman world with exquisite examples of the *Mudéjar* mastery of the horseshoe arch – these are finer than their robust, much plainer counterparts to be found in the villa patios of North Africa, revealing exquisitely carved details in the stonework.

Though the Romans are credited with inventing the arch as a weight-bearing structure, its adaptation into a more flexible horseshoe design was a Muslim refinement, one of the first successful employments of which was in the Umayyad Mosque in Damascus (AD *c.*706–715). There is some credence in the idea that it was developed originally on superstitious grounds, because of the symbolic nature of the horse-shoe (as a protector from, for example, the 'evil eye'). But the true horseshoe design, 'the arch that never sleeps', also has a practical side, since more height can be created within it than within the Classical design. The most pure examples can be seen in the Mezquita, or Great Mosque, of Abd ar-Rahman at Córdoba, where inspiration drawn from the gracefully curving canopy of the date palm tree seems as plausible as the horse's-shoe idea.

Casa de Pilatos displays the hybrid vigour of artistic styles that have mingled over centuries. One of its charms is the way it combines aesthetics drawn from Roman and Moorish precedents, along with the late-Gothic vaulting and decoration in the manner of Seville Cathedral (the latter to be seen in the chapel). The courtyard is home to various Roman statues, busts and artefacts, with more to be found in the adjoining rooms, and its walls are superbly decorated with geometric tiles of superior quality, since the local craftsmen were still actively manufacturing them; a tiled stairway leading to the apartments of the upper floor is particularly elaborate.

Further enclosed gardens, reached from the Patio Grande, are greener and less formal, with roses in box-edged beds and assorted climbers, such as fragrant jasmine and more bougainvillea, scampering over the walls. Tall palms and cycads thrive in the shelter and fountains trickle water gently in their timeless fashion.

Don Fadrique built the palace following his pilgrimage to the Holy Land between 1518 and 1520. It is said that he was so struck by the Praetorium, Pontius Pilate's official residence, that he decided to model his palace at home on it, though the name may also derive from the fact that he instituted the pious devotion of the Way of the Cross, which is still embarked upon from the Casa de Pilatos in Holy Week each year.

Above: *Finely decorated doorways link the courtyards. Various Roman artefacts – columns, busts and statues – are carefully arranged on display.*

Right: *Magenta bougainvillea straddles the wall between the entrance court and the decorated Patio Grande, though the courts are kept uncluttered.*

Above: *The central feature of the adjoining garden is a Carrara marble fountain with a nineteenth-century glorietta covered in climbing roses.*

Left: *A view into the main garden with box-edged beds and citrus and palm trees.*

MORATALLA, ANDALUCÍA

The first big surprise at Moratalla ('the Moor's lookout') is the verdancy of its landscape. The second shock, not unrelated of course, is the great size of its trees. For this is Andalucía, the deep south of Spain with its blisteringly hot summers and, for the most part, desert-dry terrain. Here, white villages cluster together like heaps of sugar cubes on parched hilltops, and magnificent black and tan bulls graze prairie-like pastures on the surrounding farms.

At Moratalla, near the Moorish city of Córdoba, there is access to unusually plentiful resources of water. The great Guadalquivir River, draining snow-melt and seasonal rains from the high sierras, flows by in its scenic valley all the way to Seville and beyond, while one of its tributaries wends another way close by Moratalla before joining the larger flow. Accordingly, there have been settlements here for millennia, and whereas the fertile hillsides of northern Algeria became the

Above: Sheets of agapanthus thrive under the massive plane trees shading the garden front of the house. Each bed is delineated by knee-high hedging.

Left: The garden courtyards and loggias provide opportunities for elegant pebble mosaic flooring.

vineyard of the Romans, this region with its vast acreages of wheat is known as Rome's breadbasket, though it has also long been a centre for olive oil and wine.

The garden's celebration (and source) of water is announced by a rock formation over which it cascades, surmounted by a statue of a proud stag. This elegant source replenishes a fountain pool which also serves as a cistern for irrigating nearby plantations of orange trees, among other things. Along the main vista, water continues to be the unifying theme, running for hundreds of yards in brick-edged rills set into an implausibly emerald-coloured lawn; along its route, little fountain jets erupt here and there out of a series of pools, including a 'puzzle' or maze channel of the sort that amused the ladies of the seraglio in the secret walled courtyards of old Moorish Spain and North Africa.

There are further surprises to come. A long vista that cuts through the gardens introduces an unexpectedly Classical French flavour, but then it turns out that most of the present gardens were designed early in the twentieth century by Jean-Claude Nicolas Forestier (1861–1930).

One of the premier landscape architects of his generation, Forestier was best known for his extensive Parisian work, which included the layout of the gardens of the Champs de Mars and restoring the Bagatelle gardens in the Bois de Boulogne, though his international practice extended across the Atlantic, with clients in Central and South America and the West Indies.

Forestier's grand vista for Moratalla, described above, was originally the formal driveway to the house, reached from an imposing iron gateway; but its conversion into a purely garden vista enforces a sense of tranquillity, with crisply sheared myrtle hedges and splendidly planted woodland gardens lining either side. As it approaches the house, the vista terminates in a large, box-edged parterre, the beds seas of blue-flowered agapanthus, with dapply shade provided by immense plane trees planted in broad arcs. The trees tower over both the house and its gardens, only fanning out branches and foliage when the trunks have reached beyond the first 50 or 60 feet. Such unexpected changes of scale bring wonder and delight into a garden that is otherwise merely

serenely beautiful. The trees also extend the flowering life of the agapanthus, cooling the atmosphere and shielding them somewhat from Andalucía's broiling summer sun. The plane trees predate Forestier's work here, for Moratalla was one of those aristocratic estates whose grounds were remodelled in the nineteenth century in the English landscape style.

Today, the gardens and the entire estate are being carefully restored and developed by the Duke of Segorbe, who bought the property in 1988 from the family of the late Marquess of Viana. The duke's initiatives permeate the grounds, not just in the high standard of upkeep, but also in the planning and planting of further areas and added pools. A carefully conceived hotel has been built within the estate, while the olive mill has been converted into a function room for events such as weddings and banquets.

Above: *Moratalla's great plane trees enclose the box-edged parterre and frame the long view.*
Right: *The garden's main vista, formerly the main driveway up to the house, is occupied by a series of Moorish-inspired fountains connected by a central rill.*

CASA POSTIGO, MADRID

La Moraleja, just 7 miles north of Madrid, is the city's most exclusive suburb, a community of substantial villas set in spacious grounds. When the Postigo house was built, in the early 1990s, Spain's leading landscape architect, Fernando Caruncho, was commissioned to design the gardens on ground that slopes away steeply behind the house. The result, after much earth-moving, is a serene series of broad terraces where few bright colours intrude on the calmness of all the greenery.

As with the Villa del Balbianello on Lake Como (*see page 134*), many different plants are shaped with the topiarist's shears so that you read the plants in the formal areas as a series of textures; flowers are purely incidental and nowhere are they the main event. At Casa Postigo, the topiaries also provide a cushioning counterpoint, lessening the extreme severity of the new stone house and its crisp flights of stairs, while always remaining orderly.

From an upper terrace, where deep porches create plenty of essential shade, open-sided stairways descend from each side of the house into the next platform of garden. Like the house, the gardens are an entirely symmetrical composition, presenting an ordered Classicism only departed from when you reach the outer gardens, which are handsomely forested. Tuscan-style terracotta pots planted with clipped box balls sit on alternate steps, defining the edge of each of these upper stairways, while the sides are covered with thick pads of closely clipped *Trachelospermum jasminoides*. This is the climbing star jasmine, whose shiny evergreen foliage is lightly dotted with a galaxy of tiny flowers that release a heady evening fragrance – an excellent choice for growing near the house. At the foot of these steps, a broad lawn with a central fountain pool appears to push away the horizons and surrounding trees,

Above: *A golden moment as santolinas erupt in the predominantly green gardens.*

Right: *The view from one of the side terraces, looking down into the lower terrace and its swimming pool. Extensive tree planting creates a verdant outlook.*

leaving instead the sensation that the sky is the most dominant part of this scheme. The garden has been thought of as a pictorial landscape image, allowing the sky to occupy two-thirds of the composition while the garden and its terrace occupy the other third.

'The sensation of the scale is very spacious, very aerial, there is a lot of sky, with a small proportion of earth,' Señor Caruncho explains. 'This sensation is accentuated by the volatile design of the stairs, which are a defining element of this project. Everything ascends and descends on the path of the stairs and the tunnel, naturally illuminated by the sun, communicating between the lower and the higher level. It feels like you are inside a dome, or on a boat in the middle of the ocean. It is this relationship between the proportions, the relationship between sky and land, that is the most important.' Fernando Caruncho is well known for the deeply philosophical approach he takes to designing his gardens, and also for drawing inspiration from Classical proportions, meticulously applied to a geometric grid. Spaces and volumes are worked out precisely from the grid, and though the results may look simple, they

Left: *The garden wall elevations are clothed with neatly clipped star jasmine,* Trachelospermum jasminoides, *bearing abundant tiny and fragrant white flowers.*

Above: *The topiarist's art is practised to an elevated degree at Postigo. Trimmed lentisc (*Pistachia lentiscus*) creates abstract shapes in contrast to the more relaxed boundaries of the garden.*

are only arrived at by careful consideration of proportions in relation to the architecture of the house. It has always been this perfect understanding of space and the manipulation of it that separates the truly great designers from the rest.

Beneath the lawn, a tunnel runs from under the centre of the house to a swimming-pool terrace on the next level down, but natural light is ingeniously allowed into the tunnel by the provision of two long rectangular grilles, bordered by hedges of neatly clipped ivy. At an intermediate level between the upper lawn and the pool terrace, there are broad platforms on either side, reached by a further pair of elegant stone stairways. Again, they are kept very open to the sky, but here each lawn has a box-enclosed parterre, of grid design, with the interstices filled with clipped grey-leaved *Santolina chamaecyparissus*. Backed on either side by six specimen trees of *Prunus serrula*, the ornamental cherry with its shiny mahogany bark, the parterres overlook the swimming-pool lawn below, but are framed on the outside by forests of pine.

The boundaries of the garden are rendered invisible by plantations of trees: pines, cypresses and cedars, which not only provide complete privacy but also give the garden the impression of being amid luxuriant, verdant countryside.

GILDEMEISTER GARDENS, MALLORCA

Riviera Nature Notes, a delightful little book published at the beginning of the last century (and recently republished), reveals the great range of plants that flourish in the Mediterranean. It is a wide-ranging collection of acute observations gathered into fascinating essays by a modest but educated cleric who signed himself merely 'C.C.'. Among the footnotes was this one, by Sir Thomas Hanbury of La Mortola (*see page 154*): 'I am disappointed if I have fewer than 450 species in flower in the open border at La Mortola in the month of January.' This single sentence sums up what the Mediterranean is capable of yielding to gardeners – at least before the heat of summer arrives.

Fast-forward to the other end of the century and we find there are many beautiful Mediterranean gardens still being made from scratch on stony hillsides; but times have changed and people are not solely focusing on winter and spring enjoyment. Today, ecology and climate are much more obviously part of the equation for anyone making a

garden, and the extreme limitations presented by thin, hungry soils, boiling-hot summers, severe restrictions on water use and the difficulty of finding skilled staff are familiar challenges.

So, at the end of 1994, the Mediterranean Garden Society was formed and among its founder members was Heidi Gildemeister, who has subsequently become known not only for the naturally beautiful garden she has created in Mallorca over many years, but also for communicating her trial-and-error experiences in several popular, practical books that have given a lifeline of hope to others. 'For the better part of the last twenty years, I have been gardening on ten acres of land on our sheep farm, which is part of the last untouched wilderness areas in the western Mediterranean,' wrote Mrs Gildemeister in *Gardening the Mediterranean Way*. 'What I discovered when we first arrived was not the plant life that had existed here a few hundred years ago. We found overgrazed fields, a neglected pine forest (*Pinus halepensis*) and the remains of a centuries-old oak forest (*Quercus ilex*). These ancient oaks became the backbone of our garden and its principal theme.'

Above: *Hemerocallis, cupressus and variegated agave provide vertical eruptions among the more rounded forms of herbs and shrubs.*

Left: *The setting is relentlessly rocky, though the hills give shelter.*

The Gildemeisters first set about repairing broken fencing to keep out foraging goats, then they nurtured seedling oaks and those stunted by grazing so that the tree canopy could be re-established. In clearing away brambles, they enabled further species of the indigenous flora to return. When *Country Life* visited Mrs Gildemeister in 1995, her garden was admired for its design, its meticulous maintenance and general plantsmanship, but most of all for 'the way it addresses one of the great questions of modern gardening – the relationship between gardening and conservation'. Mrs Gildemeister was already becoming known in horticultural circles as an authority on how to garden in an ecologically sound way, conserving both precious water and the local flora, which has its own beauty and integrity.

The Gildemeisters' land is abundantly, relentlessly rocky, though continuous applications of mulch have restored enough fertility to support hundreds of plants, both native and exotic. The natural shrub canopy includes *Viburnum tinus*, lentisc, myrtle (*Myrtus communis*) and the spiny, stout Mediterranean fan palm, *Chamaerops humilis*. 'Among

our exciting finds were two western Mediterranean endemics, *Rhamnus ludovici-salvatoris* and the spurge olive, *Cneorum tricoccon*, with its olive-like leathery leaves,' recalls Mrs Gildemeister.

Though natural contours and the muted colours of the *maquis* prevail, near the house a nod towards formal gardening is allowed, with a lawn, a terrace and pergolas draped in climbers. This is where non-native plants – colourful aeoniums of the Canary Islands, agaves from Central America and South American puyas – are allowed to predominate, alongside colourful South African species including kniphofias, osteospermums and scented-leaf pelargoniums. It is a remarkable testament to what can be achieved by taking the necessary first step of repairing the fence to keep out foraging goats.

Right: *Succulents such as echeverias and stonecrops find perfect homes in little pockets on the rockface.*

Below: *A particularly fine form of* Fatsia japonica *thrives in a holm oak's shade.*

BIBLIOGRAPHY

Abulafia, David (ed.), *The Mediterranean in History*, Thames & Hudson, London, 2003.

Agnelli, Marella, *Gardens of the Italian Villas*, Weidenfeld & Nicolson, London, 1987.

Anon., 'Maryland, Alpes Maritimes', *Country Life*, 2 January 1926.

Anon., 'A Riviera Garden: Lou Sueil', *Country Life*, 22 December 1928.

Anon., *The Villa Ephrussi de Rothschild*, Beaux Arts SA, Paris, 2002.

Aslet, Clive, 'Flor da Rosa, Portugal', *Country Life*, 15 October 1987.

Aston, Michael, *Pot Pourri*, Fondazione William Walton, Isola d'Ischia, [no date].

Atkinson, Sophie, *An Artist in Corfu*, Herbert & Daniel, London, 1911.

Baedeker, Karl, *The Mediterranean*, Karl Baedeker, Leipzig, 1911.

Bagot, R. and Ragg, L., *The Italian Lakes*, 4th edn, A. & C. Black, London, 1932.

Ballance, Margherita, 'The Garden of the Villa Cypris, Cap Martin', *Country Life*, 5 March 1927.

Balsan, Consuelo Vanderbilt, *The Glitter and The Gold*, George Mann, Maidstone, 1973.

Bazzoni, Renato, Magnifico, Marco and Dell'Orso, Silvia, *Il libro del FAI*, Skira and Fondo per l'Ambiente Italiano, Milan, 2001. FAI guidebook providing further information on Villa del Balbianello.

Benchérif, Osman, *The British in Algiers 1585–2000*, RSM Communications, Alger, 2001.

Bennet, J. Henry, *Winter and Spring on the Shores of the Mediterranean*, John Churchill & Sons, London, 1870.

Binney, Marcus, 'Casa da Insua, Beira Alta', *Country Life*, 31 May 1984.

—, *Great Houses of Europe*, Aurum Press, London, 2003.

—, 'Moratalla, Andalucía', *Country Life*, 18 July 2002.

—, 'Riviera: rescued in the nick of time', *Country Life*, 24 February 2000.

Blamey, Marjorie and Grey-Wilson, Christopher, *Mediterranean Wild Flowers*, HarperCollins, London, 1993.

Bowe, Patrick, *Gardens of the Roman World*, Frances Lincoln, London, 2004.

—, 'Natural Impact', *Country Life*, 1 June 1995.

—, 'Romantic by Every Means', *Country Life*, 26 May 1994.

Bradley-Hole, Kathryn, 'Córdoba's Secret World', *Country Life*, 30 September 2004.

—, 'Muses & Music Among the Rocks of Ages', *Country Life*, 25 October 2001.

—, 'Picture an Island Arcadia', *Country Life*, 15 August 2002.

—, 'Return to Splendour', *Country Life*, 27 October 2005.

—, *Stone, Rock and Gravel*, Cassell, London, 2000.

—, 'The Lost World of the Villa Lou Sueil', *The Mediterranean Garden*, journal of the Mediterranean Garden Society, No. 42, October 2005.

—, 'Woods of Ancient Virtue', *Country Life*, 5 May 2005.

Breger, A. M., *The Olive Tree of France*, Mexichrome, Forcalquier, 2001.

Brookes, John, *Gardens of Paradise*, Weidenfeld & Nicolson, London, 1987.

Brown, Jane, *Eminent Gardeners*, Viking, London, 1990.

Bucknall, Stephen A., *Benjamin Joseph Bucknall, disciple of Viollet-le-Duc*, Minerva, Transactions of the Royal Institution of South Wales, Volume II.

Cameron, Roderick, *The Golden Riviera*, Weidenfeld & Nicolson, London, 1975.

Campanelli, Daniela (ed.), *Il Monastero di Santa Chiara*, Electa, Naples, 1995.

Carita, Hender and Cardoso, António Homem (photographer), *Portuguese Gardens*, Antique Collectors' Club, Woodbridge, 1990.

Cassy, Rob (ed.), *Riviera Nature Notes* [edited version of original title by 'C.C.' in 1903], Signal Books, Oxford, 2004.

Cleveland-Peck, Patricia, 'Verdi Act Tree', *Country Life*, 3 July 2003.

Cooper, Diana, *Trumpeters from the Steep*, Century, London, 1984.

Cooper, Guy and Taylor, Gordon, *Mirrors of Paradise: the gardens of Fernando Caruncho*, The Monacelli Press, New York, 2000.

Conway, Martin, 'Crowherst [sic] Place, Surrey, III', *Country Life*, 19 July 1919.

Cox, E. H. M., 'La Leopolda', *Country Life*, 19 January 1929.

—, 'Lou Sueil I, Éze, A.M.', *Country Life*, 5 February 1927.

—, 'Lou Sueil II, Éze, A.M.', *Country Life*, 12 February 1927.

—, 'Sainte-Claire le Château, Hyères', *Country Life*, 3 November 1928.

—, 'Villa Sylvia, Cap Ferrat', *Country Life*, 15 January 1927.

Craig, Theresa, *Edith Wharton: A House Full of Rooms*, The Monacelli Press, New York, 1996.

Credland, Arthur G., *The Wilson Line*, Tempus Publishing, Stroud, 2000.

De'Medici, Lorenza, *The Renaissance of Italian Gardens*, Pavilion, London, 1990.

Doutt, Richard L., *Cape Bulbs*, B. T. Batsford, London, 1994.

Dwight, Eleanor, *Edith Wharton: An Extraordinary Life*, Harry N. Abrams, New York, 1994.

Facaros, Dana and Pauls, Michael, *Granada, Seville, Córdoba*, Cadogan Guides, London, 2003.

—, *Lombardy & The Italian Lakes*, Cadogan Guides, London, 2003.

Fell, Derek, *Renoir's Garden*, Simon & Schuster, New York, 1991.

Festing, Sally, *Gertrude Jekyll*, Viking, London, 1991.

Fine Art Society, *Eastern Encounters: Orientalist Painters of the Nineteenth Century*, London, 1978.

Flament, Albert, '*Une belle demeure fleurie*', *L'Illustration*, 2 April 1932.

Forsyth, Alastair, 'The Grand Hotel Afloat: Cunard's Maritime Masterpieces', *Country Life*, 26 December 1985.

Fromentin, Eugène, *Une Année dans le Sahel*, Bibliothèque Contemporaine, Paris, 1859.

Fussell, Paul, *Abroad*, Oxford University Press, Oxford, 1980.

Gildemeister, Heidi, *Gardening the Mediterranean Way*, Thames & Hudson, London, 2004.

—, *Mediterranean Gardening: A Waterwise Approach*, University of California Press, 2002.

Griffiths, Mark, *The Royal Horticultural Society Index of Garden Plants*, Macmillan, London, 1994.

Hall, Michael, 'Les Collettes, Cagnes-sur-Mer', *Country Life*, 13 July 1995.

Hanbury, Cecil, 'La Mortola, Ventimiglia, Italy', *Country Life*, 11 February 1928.

Haslam, Richard, 'Sant' Antonio, Tivoli', *Country Life*, 22 November 2001.

Henderson, John, *Hortus: The Roman Book of Gardening*, Routledge, London, 2004.

Herbert, Lady, *Algeria: A Search after Sunshine in 1871*, Richard Bentley & Son, London, 1872.

Hirsch, Pam, *Barbara Leigh Smith Bodichon: Feminist, Artist and Rebel*, Chatto & Windus, London, 1998.

Hobhouse, Penelope, *Gardens of Italy*, Mitchell Beazley, London, 1998.

—, *Gardens of Persia*, Cassell, London, 2003.

Hyam, Joseph C., *The Illustrated Guide to Algiers*, Anglo-French Press Association, Paris, 1899.

Ingram, Collingwood, *A Garden of Memories*, Witherby Ltd, London, 1970.

Jekyll, Gertrude, *Wood and Garden*, Longmans, Green & Co, London, 1899.

Jepson, Tim, *The Explorer Guide to Portugal*, AA Publishing, Farnborough, Hampshire, 2005.

Johnson, A. E., 'Country Life in Greece', *Country Life*, 20 September 1913.

Johnston, Shirley and Schezen, Roberto, *Great Villas of the Riviera*, Rizzoli, New York, 1998.

Jones, Louisa, *Gardens of the French Riviera*, Flammarion, Paris, 1994.

Jones, Ted, *The French Riviera, A Literary Guide for Travellers*, I. B. Tauris, London, 2004.

Klein, H., 'A Djenan-Ali-Raïs', *Feuillets d'El-Djezaïr*, 1910.

Kuttner, Ann, 'Delight and Danger in the Roman Water Garden' in *Landscape Design and the Experience of Motion*, ed. Michel Conan, Dumbarton Oaks, Washington DC, 2003.

Latymer, Hugo, *The Mediterranean Gardener*, Frances Lincoln/Royal Botanical Gardens, Kew, London, 2001.

Lees-Milne, Alvilde, 'Lawrence Johnston, Creator of Hidcote Garden' in *By Pen & By Spade: Garden Writing from Hortus*, ed. David Wheeler, Sutton, Stroud, 1990.

Leigh Fermor, Patrick, *Mani: Travels in the Southern Peloponnese*, John Murray, London, 1958.

Lucifero, Roberto and Berliocchi, Luigi, *Guida ai giardini perduti di Roma*, TECLA, Rome, 1995.

Mackenzie Stuart, Amanda, *Consuelo & Alva: Love and Power in the Gilded Age*, HarperCollins, London, 2005.

Magnus, Maurice, *Memoirs of the Foreign Legion*, Secker & Warburg, London, 1924.

March Phillipps, E., *The Gardens of Italy*, ed. Arthur T. Bolton, Country Life, London, 1919.

Marinelli, Janet (ed.), *Plant*, Dorling Kindersley/Royal Botanic Gardens, Kew, London, 2004.

Martineau, Mrs Philip, *Gardening in Sunny Lands*, Richard Cobden-Sanderson, London, 1924.

Mencos, Eduardo, *Hidden Gardens of Spain*, Frances Lincoln, London, 2004.

Miles, P., 'The Garden at the Villa Noailles, France', *The Garden*, September 1977.

Ministère de l'agriculture et du developpement rural, *Bref Historique du Jardin d'essais du Hamma*, Algerian government paper, 2004.

Moore, Alasdair, *La Mortola in the footsteps of Thomas Hanbury*, Cadogan Guides, London, 2004.

Nelson, Michael, *Queen Victoria and the Discovery of the Riviera*, I. B. Tauris & Co, London, 2001.

Ottewill, David, *The Edwardian Garden*, Yale University Press, New Haven & London, 1989.

Page, Russell, *The Education of a Gardener*, Collins, London, 1962.

Pankhurst, Alex, *Who Does Your Garden Grow?*, Earl's Eye Publishing, Colchester, 1992.

Passino, Carla, 'In the Cloister Garden Beats a Pagan Heart', *Country Life*, 8 July 2004.

Paterson-Jones, Colin, *The Cape Floral Kingdom*, New Holland, London, 1997.

Pearson, Susan and Pearson, Graham, 'The Hunt for Hidcote's Horticultural Treasures', *Country Life*, 19 February 2004.

Pemble, John, *The Mediterranean Passion*, Oxford University Press, Oxford, 1988.

Playfair, Sir R. Lambert, *Murray's Handbook for Travellers in Algeria and Tunis*, 5th edn, John Murray, London, 1895.

Quest-Ritson, Charles, *The English Garden Abroad*, Penguin, London, 1996.

Racine, M., Boursier-Mougenot, E. J.-P. and Binet, F., *The Gardens of Provence and the French Riviera*, The MIT Press, Cambridge, Massachusetts, 1987.

Reads Nursery, *Catalogue of Citrus, Figs, Grapevines and other fruits*, Loddon, Norfolk, 2004.

Richardson, Tim, *English Gardens in the Twentieth Century*, Aurum Press, London, 2005.

—, 'Moorish Balms', *Country Life*, 25 April 1996.

—, 'Paradise Set Against the Sky', *Country Life*, 18 July 2002.

Ross, Christopher, *Montfeld*, unpublished historical notes gathered in 1989–91.

Rothschild, M., Garton, K. and de Rothschild, L., *The Rothschild Gardens*, Gaia Books, London, 1996.

Russell, Vivian, *Gardens of the Riviera*, Little, Brown, London, 1993.

Scott, Philippa, *Turkish Delights*, Thames & Hudson, London, 2001.

Segall, Barbara, *Gardens of Spain & Portugal*, Mitchell Beazley, London, 1999.

Séguin, L. G., *Walks in Algiers and its Surroundings*, Daldy, Isbister & Co., London, 1878.

Strong, Roy, *Country Life 1897–1997: The English Arcadia*, Boxtree, London, 1996.

Tankard, Judith, 'Where Flowers Bloom in the Sands', *Country Life*, 12 March 1998.

Thacker, Christopher, *The History of Gardens*, Croom Helm, London, 1979.

Theodoridis, Panos, *The Olive in Greece*, Natural History Museum of the Lesvos Petrified Forest/Topio Publications, Smyrni, Greece, 2001.

Theroux, Paul, *The Pillars of Hercules*, Penguin, London, 1996.

Tipping, H. Avray, 'Maryland I, Alpes Maritimes', *Country Life*, 3 December 1910.

—, 'Maryland II, Alpes Maritimes', *Country Life*, 10 December 1910.

—, 'The Villa Sylvia, Alpes Maritimes', *Country Life*, 16 July 1910.

Trehane, Jennifer, *Camellias*, B. T. Batsford, London, 1998.

Triggs, H. Inigo, 'Ancient Arab Houses and Gardens: Djenan-el-Mufti and El Bardo', *Country Life*, 18 September 1915.

Turner, Tom, *Garden History: Philosophy and Design, 2000BC–2000AD*, Spon Press, Abingdon, 2005.

Upson, Tim and Andrews, Susyn, *The Genus Lavandula*, Royal Botanic Gardens, Kew, 2004.

Walet, Marie and Vidal-Bué, Marion, *Les peintres de l'autre rive*, Musée de la Castre, Cannes, 2003.

Walton, Susana, *La Mortella: An Italian Garden Paradise*, New Holland, London, 2002.

—, *La Mortella: the place of myrtles*, Fondazione William Walton, Isola d'Ischia, [no date].

Waters, Helena L., *The French & Italian Rivieras*, Methuen & Co., London, 1924.

Watkin, David, 'Cavogallo, Southern Peloponnese', *Country Life*, 9 February 1995.

Wharton, Edith, *Italian Villas and their Gardens*, The Century Co., New York, 1904.

—, *The Cruise of the Vanadis*, Bloomsbury, London, 2004.

Whitsey, Fred, 'Where Wharton Led ...', *Country Life*, 7 July 1994.

USEFUL ADDRESSES

The following gardens are regularly open to visitors

ALGERIA

El Bardo (Musée National du Bardo)
03 rue F. D. Roosevelt
16000 Telemly
Algiers
Tel: (02) 74 76 41

FRANCE

Sainte-Claire le Château
Avenue Edith Wharton
83400 Hyères-les-Palmiers

Les Collettes (Domaine des Collettes)
Chemin des Collettes
06800 Cagnes-sur-Mer
Tel: (0)4 93 20 61 07

Villa Île de France
(Villa Ephrussi de Rothschild)
Avenue E. de Rothschild
06230 Saint-Jean-Cap-Ferrat
Tel: (0)4 93 01 33 09
Fax: (0)4 93 01 31 10
www.villa-ephrussi.com

Villa Noailles
Parc St-Bernard
Montée de Noailles
83400 Hyères-les-Palmiers

Jardin Serre de la Madone
74 Route de Gorbio
06500 Menton
Tel: (0)4 93 57 73 90
www.serredelamadone.com

ITALY

Villa del Balbianello
22016 Lenno
Balbianello Villa
Via Comoedia
22016 Lenno
Como
Tel: (0)3 44 56 110
www.fondoambiente.it

Villa Doria Pamphilj
(Casino del Bel Respiro)
Piazzetta del Bel Respiro
00165 Rome

Villa Gregoriana
Tivoli
Rome
Tel: (0)6 39 96 77 01

Villa Hanbury
(Giardini Botanici Hanbury)
Corso Montecarlo 43
18038 La Mortola Inferiore
Ventimiglia
Tel. (0184) 22 95 07

Isola Madre
28838 Stresa (Verbania)
Tel. (0)3 23 / 31 261
www.borromeoturismo.it

La Mortella
Fondazione William Walton e
La Mortella
via F. Calise 39
80075 Forio
Isola d'Ischia
Naples
Tel. (0)81 98 62 20
E-mail: info@lamortella.it

Cloister of Santa Chiara
Strada Santa Chiara
Quartiere di Spacca-Napoli
Naples

PORTUGAL

Casa da Insua
Penalva do Castelo
Beira Alta

SPAIN

Casa de Pilatos
Plaza de Pilatos 1
Seville
Tel. 95 422 52 98
www.sevilla5.com/monuments/pilatos.html

Jardín de Moratalla
La carretera de Posadas
Córdoba
Andalucía

INDEX